INTERNATIONAL
CLASSIC CAR
YEAR

1996 - 1997

On the left, the McLaren F1 road car. 6.1 litre normally aspirated V12 engine. 0-60mph in 3.2 seconds. 103bhp per litre.

On the right, the new BMW M3 Evolution.

3.2 litre normally aspirated straight six engine. 0-60mph in 5.3 seconds. 100.3 bhp per litre.

It is no coincidence that these two extraordinary engines both offer the elusive 100bhp

per litre. For they both also carry the name BMW M Power.

Since its inception in 1972, the BMW motorsport division has rewritten many engineering

THE M3 EVOLUTION PRICES, CORRECT AT TIME OF GOING TO PRESS, START FROM £37,460, INCLUDE VAT, EXCLUDE ROAD FUND LICENCE AND, AT AN ESTIMATED COST OF £470, DELIVERY AND NUMBER

YOU WAIT YEARS FOR AN ENGINE TO BREAK 100 BHP PER LITRE. THEN TWO COME ALONG TOGETHER.

rules. Not to mention record books. And in so doing has helped create some of the world's most revered cars. (In the 1995 Le Mans 24 hour race, the F1 won and took 4 of the top 5 places.)

Small wonder then that the M3 Evolution has the critics swooning.

Autocar magazine summed up the feelings of its press colleagues when it used the phrase "...a mind-blowing supercar..."†

Very kind, but we can't help thinking we've heard that before somewhere.

THE ULTIMATE DRIVING MACHINE

PLATES. BMW INFORMATION: PO BOX 161, CROYDON, SURREY, CR9 1QB. FREEPHONE 0800 325600; INTERNET http://www.bmw.co.uk TAX-FREE SALES CALL 0171 409 3355. †AUTOCAR. 09/08/95.

CONTENTS

EDITOR Brian Laban **ASSOCIATE EDITOR** Kevin Brazendale **ART DIRECTOR** Martin Chappell **DESIGNER** Rob Patterson
MARKETING MANAGER Nick Peart **SECRETARY** Sue August **SALES DIRECTOR** Alan Talbot **PUBLISHING DIRECTOR** Terry Griffiths
MANAGING DIRECTOR Terry Humphreys **PRODUCTION CO-ORDINATOR** Neville Lloyd
COLOUR ORIGINATION Rapida Group plc **PRINTED AND BOUND** P S Colour Limited

First published in Great Britain in 1996, by XL Communications Limited, Warwick House, Cowcross Street, London EC1M 6BP
Copyright © 1996 XL Communications Limited ISBN - 0 952895900

Fast, but we keep it quiet.

powered by
mtu

Considering it does up to 41 knots, with a cruising range of up to 400 nautical miles, the twin diesel engined *Predator 63* is remarkably quiet about it. That's because we've fitted her with super-efficient shaft drives to keep any noise and vibration to a minimum. This, plus the latest navigation aids and a 14' Outlaw sportsboat housed beneath the sun-lounger, all make this a vessel we think you'll like the sound of.

Sunseeker

Sunseeker International Limited, 27-31 West Quay Road, Poole, Dorset, England BH15 1HX. Telephone: +44 (0)1202 381111, Fax +44 (0)1202 382222

Sunseeker International Limited. Sunseeker design and construct a range of 17 innovative and distinctive craft.

BREITLING
1884

CROSSWIND

BREITLING's new mechanical super-chronograph displays exceptional styling refinement for a wrist instrument of such technical character. Its sweeping lines and exclusive design features express the spirit of luxury built in to the grandly conceived CROSSWIND.

High-flying excellence

Designed to meet the stringent requirements of air navigation, the CROSSWIND chronograph measures and records times to a maximum of 12 hours, including intermediate and cumulative times, with 1/5th second precision.

The CROSSWIND is available in steel, with twin-metal finish or in solid 18 K gold, fitted with a leather strap or a PILOT bracelet.

AVAILABLE FROM SELECTED JEWELLERS THROUGHOUT GREAT BRITAIN AND IRELAND.
FOR YOUR NEAREST STOCKIST TELEPHONE 0171 637 5167

INSTRUMENTS FOR PROFESSIONALS

Lord Montagu of Beaulieu

FOREWORD

The sporting side of the classic car world has grown considerably over recent years, until it now offers a large number of competitive events and exciting championships - each of which produces excellent racing but which still broadly enjoy the kind of back to basics atmosphere which reminds one of the days when motor racing was mostly for fun, and largely unspoiled by today's twin evils of politics and money.

I have long been involved in furthering the interests of the classic and historic car world, and especially that of Britain's own motoring heritage, so I am delighted to be asked to write this foreword to the first book of its kind, devoted solely to the more prestigious classic and historic motoring events of the past year - in superb photographic detail with words which mix the colour, excitement, quality and passion of the subject.

At Beaulieu, we host numerous events each year, from club events to our international Autojumble, which is now entering its fourth decade. And I, like you am a keen follower of everything from the great road races to traditional concours - in all of which, intense competition gives pleasure to participant and spectator alike.

I welcome International Classic Car Year, and trust that like me you will enjoy 1996 through its pages, while looking forward to another fine year in 1997.

Montagu of Beaulieu

There's never been a dull Aston Martin

We're about to reveal our small, but significant, contribution to the glittering history of one of the most illustrious names in British motoring.

For nearly three decades, new Aston Martins have left Newport Pagnell with an Autoglym shine. If that comes as a surprise, then here's something else that may intrigue you.

Because of its service and special projects expertise, the Customer Service Division at Newport Pagnell attracts even not-so-new Aston Martins from all over the World. After receiving anything from a little tender loving care to a full restoration, they always leave with the added protection of Autoglym as a shining reminder of a classic tradition.

If you'd like to follow this fine example, you'll find a complete range of Autoglym's easy to use, car care products at all discerning car accessory shops.

Of course, you may not be fortunate enough to own an Aston Martin, but that's no reason why you should ever be seen driving a dull car.

BY APPOINTMENT TO
H.M. QUEEN ELIZABETH THE QUEEN MOTHER
SUPPLIER OF CAR CARE PRODUCTS
AUTOGLYM, LETCHWORTH, ENGLAND

BY APPOINTMENT TO
H.R.H. THE PRINCE OF WALES
SUPPLIER OF CAR CARE PRODUCTS
AUTOGLYM, LETCHWORTH, ENGLAND

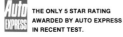 THE ONLY 5 STAR RATING
AWARDED BY AUTO EXPRESS
IN RECENT TEST.

AUTOGLYM, WORKS ROAD, LETCHWORTH, HERTS, SG6 1LU. TEL: 01462 677766 FAX: 677712

Brian Laban - Editor

INTRODUCTION

Like Lord Montagu, I have enjoyed a good deal of satisfaction in watching the steady growth of both public and mainstream motor industry interest in the world of classic cars in general and in classic motor sport in particular. Over the past four or five years, the classic marketplace has regained something of a sense of sanity, while historic racing has moved a long way from its one-time role of supporting act or second feature. In fact it has grown to the point where now, with events as diverse as the Mille Miglia and the Goodwood Festival of Speed, it attracts crowds that wouldn't disgrace a modern Grand Prix, while enticing sponsors of the calibre of, say, Chrysler, Coys and Louis Vuitton, Chopard and Shell.

The very existence of this first edition of International Classic Car Year reflects that growth in popularity, and we hope it also celebrates it.

It is starting from zero, with what we hope is a long future ahead of it. It is international in the true sense, in that it covers events the world over, but it in no way claims to be comprehensive. Even for an annual, that would need something the size of Britannica, and it wasn't our aim. For sheets of results and the small details of every weekend's action, you should look elsewhere: our ambition is more to capture the spirit and the atmosphere of our subject, in words and in pictures. We hope you approve.

Last of the Great Texas Land Dynasties

Recently featured on *Lifestyles of the Rich and Famous*, this is distinguished as the epitome of a palatial Texas Ranch – a huge , sprawling, luxurious compound set against a wide open landscape and bright blue sky.

Boasting one of the finest show horse facilities in the world, the ranch is host to many prestigious cutting horse shows. A spectacular 65,000 square foot arena is lavishly equipped for entertaining with the elaborate Cutter's Cantina, a lounge and club that can accommodate 500 persons. The arena includes a 36,000 square foot, dirt-floored working area, a five office complex, grandstands, an announcer's booth, electronic scoreboard, laundry and tack rooms, staff housing, and 41 stalls with running water, individual heaters and ceiling fans. An adjacent mare barn offers 60 additional similar stalls, and eight more are located in a nearby stud barn.

This ranch commands nearly 3,000 acres with frontage on both the Nueces River and Espantosa Creek and has a beautiful 1,200 acre game preserve stocked with trophy native and exotic wildlife, a three acre bass lake, and two catfish ponds for excellent fishing.

The main house itself seems made for entertaining huge numbers of guests – up to 1,000. And up to 57 guests can easily be accomodated overnight in the utmost luxury in three three-bedroom guest houses, three three- and two-bedroom modular homes, plus numerous guest facilities and suites. These, along with extensive staff quarters, are all completely furnished.

Introduced by an impressive drive lined with over 300 stately pecan trees, the Spanish-style stucco main residence is truly one of a kind. Throughout the residence (approximately the size of a football field), nearly everything is custom-designed and built to exacting standards. Highlights include four grand fireplaces, an ornate game room and den complete with bar, a commercial-grade gourmet kitchen, walk-in freezer and walk-in wine storage cooler, an elevator, numerous works of fine art, plus countless other luxurious amenities. The residence opens to an enormous swimming pool and cascading waterfall surrounded by a flagstone patio, poolside bar, veranda, and beautiful gardens.

This truly exceptional property includes all real property, improvements and available minerals, equipment, furnishings, and art work.

Hoffman Realty Inc. 214-698-1736

Hoffman Realty Sells World Class Property

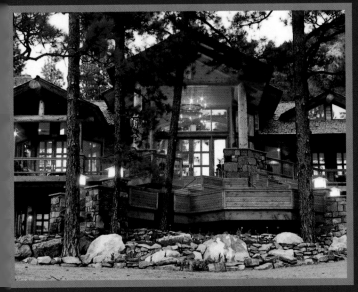

COLORADO SHOWPLACE – Prime location near Durango, spectacular 8,000' home, 2 guest homes, barn, arena and beautiful mountain views.

GRAND CAYMAN ISLANDS - Magnificent custom 2 storey villa on the golf course at the Britannia Resort at Seven Mile Beach. All the amenities of the Hyatt Regency Resort are yours, including gourmet dining in 3 restaurants, room service, health club, private beach with a world class diving operation, and all hotel and banquet services.

SCOTTISH LANDMARK CASTLE – Turreted Castle with 16th century origins., restored to perfection. 6 Reception Rooms, 15 Bedrooms, 7 Baths, 90 acres.

Membership is included in the unique Jack Nicklaus designed golf course. Professionally decorated with custom furnishings which are included in the sale, this villa comes with a lavishly appointed 40' Carver Voyager yacht for only $1,295,000 U.S. Dollars. Or the villa is offered without the yacht for only $1,095,000 U.S. Dollars.

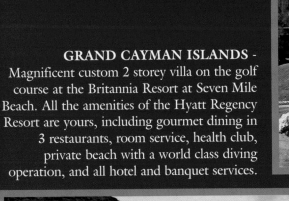

PARADISE VALLEY, ARIZONA – A spectacular mountainside home on 8 acres with incredible views of Camelback Mountain. Offered at $2,400,000. U.S. Dollars.

SPRINGFIELD, MISSOURI – 55 acres with a 4 story, 20,000' Tudor Manor, stables, pool and house, guesthouse and courts. Offered at $4,500,000 U.S. Dollars.

Hoffman Realty Inc. 214-698-1736

Dallas, TX	214-698-1736	Philadelphia, PA	215-592-8109
Dallas - Fax	214-823-2350	Lake Tahoe-Reno, NV	888-338-4664
New York, NY	800-648-1736	Toronto, ONT	416-760-4328
Beverly Hills, CA	213-855-0384	San Clemente, CA	714-492-3512
Santa Barbara, CA	805-966-0219	Middleburg, VA	703-687-3058
Palm Springs, CA	619-341-9727	Newport Beach, CA	714-675-1931
Washington, DC	202-638-2033	Charlottesville, VA	804-973-1572

Your *Ultimate*
Car deserves...
...the Ultimate
Cover

John Scott Insurance Brokers
has a strong and long standing
reputation of looking after
the special insurance
needs of classic car
owners, collectors
and dealers.

For the Right Cover
at the Right Price,
talk to Us First...

John Scott Insurance Brokers

Briarcliff House, Kingsmead, Farnborough, Hampshire GU14 7TE Telephone: 01252 807300 *Facsimile: 01252 801520*
John Scott Insurance Brokers is part of Aon UK, A Division of Aon Risk Services UK Limited.

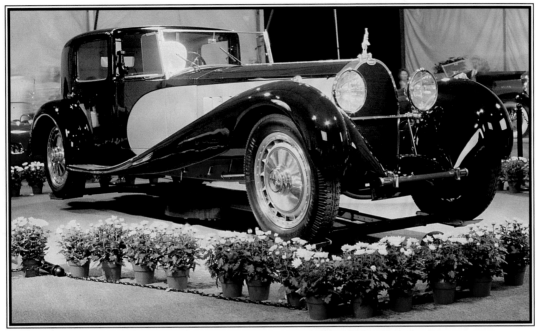

Bugatti Royale at Barrett Jackson in January was year's first disappointment, failing to reach $14 million reserve

WINTER

*1996 started with a significant New Year's present for
many British old-car enthusiasts, in the year in which
the British motor industry would officially, and fairly
extensively, celebrate its centenary. But it wasn't only in
Britain that classic car culture was showing its influence
on present, and even future motoring. Just think Retro.*

1 January
*Following Kenneth Clarke's November budget, UK classic
car enthusiasts now enjoy tax concessions on most vehicles of
more than 25 years old. Mr Clarke believes 'the exemption
produces a generous and coherent system of taxation for older
vehicles and reflects the important role old vehicle enthusiasts
play in maintaining this vibrant part of our heritage. . .'*

3 January
*Today's concept car is the day after tomorrow's classic. At the
Detroit Show, Ford design boss Jack Telnak described the
Lincoln Sentinel as being 'designed to win the Concours
d'Elegance at Pebble Beach in 50 years time'. Sentinel, with
its 'Edge Design', is latest in a growing line of retro-evoca-
tive designs, a large luxury car harking back (in Ford's own*

*words) to classics like the 1961 Lincoln Continental and the
Facel Vega Excellence.*

3 January
*Terrence Cuneo, motoring artist and painter of the famous
picture of Woolf Barnato's Bentley racing the Blue Train in
the 1930s, has died, at the age of 89.*

4 January
*At the Detroit Show, Ford confirms that former world cham-
pion Jackie Stewart's new Grand Prix team will have Ford
support from its launch in 1997.*

11 January
Scottsdale '96 auction included a 1940 Mercedes Benz

770K, described as 'the first Grosser Mercedes delivered to the Third Reich' - former user von Ribbentrop. In the UK, Coys of Kensington auctioned the world's oldest surviving Austin Seven Mini, from 1959, for an amazing £11,800

12 January

Jaguar chairman Nick Scheele hosted a dinner for more than 350 guests in the company museum, to celebrate 45 years of competition and seven wins at Le Mans, and to support the Jaguar Heritage Trust. The menu included Saumon Fumé Arnage and Medaillons de Boeuf Mulsanne; guests included Paul Frère, Jack Fairman, John Watson, Tom Walkinshaw, Jan Lammers, Derek Warwick and Norman Dewis - chief test driver of the ill-fated XJ13 which took centre stage at the dinner alongside many of the cars that Jaguar did race at Le Mans.

14 January

Maurice 'Mo' Gomm, metal worker and racing car chassis builder extraordinary, and the man who built all the early Ralt racing chassis, died, aged 74.

18 January

The service in Coventry Cathedral celebrating the centenary of the British motor industry started with the arrival of an 1896 Daimler, ended with the departure of a Coventry built electrically propelled Peugeot, and was interrupted in mid-flight by a modern Lady Godiva who removed her fur coat to reveal she was wearing nothing more than a few daubed-on anti-car slogans.

20 January

It is 100 years today since the first British speeding ticket was issued, to Walter Arnold of Kent, who was caught by a policeman on a bicycle after a half-hour chase for exceeding the 2mph limit. He pleaded not guilty and was fined a token amount.

24 January

It is reported that the Bugatti trademark is up for sale, by Bugatti's beleagured owner Romano Artioli - but the Bugatti company's receiver is less than happy, as the famous trademark is one of the cash-strapped group's few obvious assets.

29 February

Christies have sold a 1:12.5 scale model of the first Beetle for just over £42,000. The model is one of a series of five, built in 1938 at the Porsche Apprentice School and with incredible detail under its lift-off body - including working suspension, steering and driveshafts, plus full trim and carpeting. The models were originally presented to leading players in VW's creation; number one went to one A Hitler, number two to Beetle designer Dr Porsche, and this one to Dr Robert Bosch, as an eightieth birthday present. The 1996 buyer, appropriately enough, was the Bosch Electronics company. Also during this week, Aussie writer, broadcaster and motor racing enthusiast Clive James, on his TV show, described a Formula One car as 'a piece of modern sculpture propelled by burning money'

5 March

At the Geneva Show, VW officially christen the retro-styled

Concept 1 first shown in Detroit in 1994 the Beetle! Renault also join the fast growing show-car nostalgia trail, at the far end of the scale from the Lincoln Sentinel, shown at Detroit, with the diminutive Fiftie, above - a retro styled coupe celebrating the fiftieth anniversary of the 4CV and based on the new Renault Sport Spyder. And Jaguar finally unveils the XK8 - successor to the long-running XJ-S V12, as laid to rest in January. It makes no secret of its evocation of classic sporting Jaguars gone by, including the E-type, launched 35 years ago virtually to the day.

5 March

Fritz Huschke von Hanstein died, aged 85. Educated in Germany and at Oxford, the German aristocrat won the 1940 Mille Miglia in a BMW 328, and joined Porsche in 1952 to become a long serving and much admired racing team manager and amiable PR boss.

6 March

Autocar magazine reports (perhaps a little prematurely but ultimately accurately) that Korean car giant and name-in-the-news Daewoo is about to buy the ailing Lotus company from equally troubled Bugatti chief Romano Artioli. Both classic names seem to be hovering on the brink of extinction.

15 March

Aiming to guarantee its future world championship status, the organisers of the modern Monte Carlo Rally hint that they may abandon the event's traditional Concentration Run section for 1997 - one of modern rallying's last links with the old format.

20 March

Donington owner Tom Wheatcroft's 'new' Bugatti Royale, a 7-year labour of love comprising 99 per cent new parts (including the entire engine) is unveiled at Goodwood House at the preview for the Festival of Speed. The car has already covered more than 2000 miles and is due to be offered for sale at the Kruse auction in May - with an expected minimum asking price of $3.5 million. It is also reported today that Carroll Shelby is threatening the receiver of AC Cars with legal action over their description of the company (again up for sale) as manufacturer of the AC Cobra. Shelby insists Shelby America, not AC, built Cobras.

31 March

Dante Giacosa, father of the Topolino and one of Fiat's greatest engineers, died, aged 91. He created the 500A Topolino in 1936 at the beginning of a fifty-year design career with Fiat, and followed it up in 1957 with the next generation Fiat baby car, the Nuova 500. He also created other Fiat classics. ranging from the company's first front-wheel-drive car, the 128, to the fast and sporting eight-cylinder 8V and the elegant and luxurious 130 - styled by Pininfarina and propelled by Fiat's version of the Ferrari Dino V6 engine, bumping up the numbers for racing homologation and production economy.

100 Years

In the 100 years since Emancipation Day took the shackles off the early motorists, the British motor industry has achieved a vast amount. BRIAN LABAN looks at some of the highlights

When the motor car came to Britain, Victoria was queen, Gladstone was prime minister. The Empire still circled the globe. When the notorious 'Red Flag Act' of 1865 was repealed, the automobile, until then hounded by the law and reviled by the horse-loving establishment, looked forward to freedom and respectability.

That came in November 1896, whereafter it was no longer necessary for a man (with or without a red flag) to walk in front of any self-propelled vehicle, and when the speed limit on Britain's open roads was raised to a heady 12mph. The repeal of the Red Flag Act was celebrated (while Kitchener was fighting in Sudan) by the first 'Emancipation Day' run from London to Brighton.

But 1996 marked an even more important centenary too, because 1896 also saw the first faltering steps of the British motor industry. Few cars had been built in Britain before shadowy entrepreneur Henry Lawson founded the British Daimler Company in Coventry in 1896 - and through his Great Horseless Carriage Company set out to hold the fledgling industry to ransom, by dubious patents and punitive royalties.

The monopoly was soon broken however, and by the time

As the Daily Chronicle wrote, 'the little town of Reigate was all agog' on Emancipation Day, above left, watching cars celebrate the end of the man with the red flag. Since then Britain has taken the Land Speed Record 24 times and Thrust, right, still held it in 1996

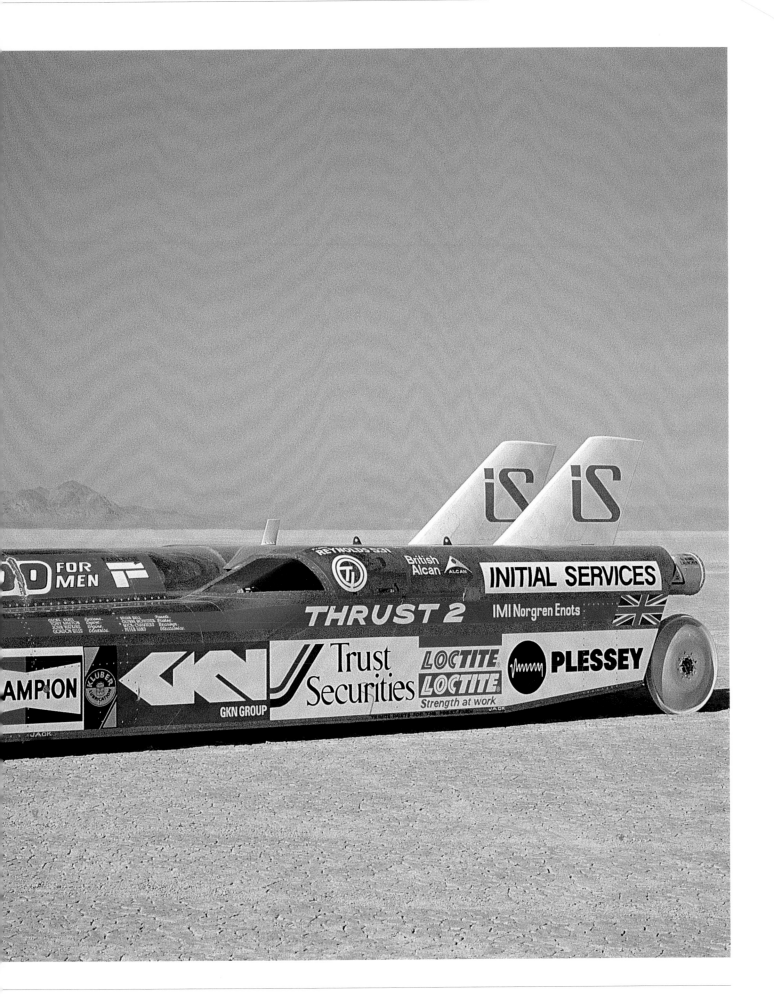

Britain had the world's first purpose built motor racing circuit. Brooklands opened in 1907 and it was intended to help motor manufacturers develop better cars as well as to foster British motor racing skills

the Boer War broke out in 1899, companies like Sunbeam and Wolseley were building cars alongside their bicycles and sheep shearing equipment. In 1900 the 1000 Miles Trial demonstrated the motor car's growing practicality. In 1903 Edward VII (Britain's first royal motorist) became Emperor of India, the speed limit reached 20mph, registration numbers and driving licences were introduced, and London marine engineers the Vauxhall Iron Works built their first car. In 1904 the first electric train ran on the London underground, Mr Rolls met Mr Royce and bicycle makers Rover became car makers - a year before one Herbert Austin left Wolseley to start his own company.

By 1907, when the Boy Scout movement was founded and the Lusitania took the Blue Riband for the fastest Atlantic crossing, there were more than 60,000 cars in Britain and Rolls-Royce's first Silver Ghost ('The Best Car in the World') had completed a 15,000-mile run with only one unscheduled stop. When the Brooklands circuit near Weybridge opened in 1907, it was the first purpose built motor racing track in the world. And for three decades it was one of the greatest motoring venues in the world - cradle for the industry, and especially for its sporting names, from five-times Le Mans winners Bentley, to record breakers Vauxhall, and affordable sports cars such as Riley and MG, which peppered the ranks of British car makers between the wars.

In 1911 the Siege of Sydney Street grabbed the headlines, and the Ford Motor Company opened a factory in Manchester to become Britain's biggest car maker. In 1912 William Morris (later Lord Nuffield) introduced his 10hp Morris Oxford and by

1914 there were some 200 makes on the British market - mostly destined for short, turbulent lives.

Between the wars the industry enjoyed worldwide sales and quaint domestic rules. In 1920 car-tax increased but pre-1914 cars paid half and a car was exempt altogether if it was used only for taking servants to church or voters to the polls. The 3-litre Bentley was launched in 1921 while cinema-goers swooned to Rudi Valentino. It was followed a year later by its antithesis, the Austin 7, as Marconi first tried a wireless receiver in a Daimler. In 1923 a policeman on a white horse averted disaster at the FA Cup Final and MG and Triumph built their first sports cars.

Traffic lights appeared in London in 1926 but traffic was stopped anyway by the General Strike. A pattern of takeovers and mergers began. Wolseley was bought by Morris; Rootes bought Hillman and Humber; Rolls-Royce bought bankrupt Bentley. Cars were becoming cheaper: in 1931 Morris introduced a spartan 8hp two-seater for just £100 - a price matched by Ford's 8hp by 1935, as transport minister Hoare Belisha introduced driving tests, the 30mph limit and pedestrian crossings.

In 1937 the Motor Show moved from Olympia (where it had been held since 1905) to Earls Court; petrol went up from 8d to 9d a gallon. Come 1940, manufacture was turned over entirely to war work, and in November Coventry was blitzed.

After the war, SS Cars decided that in light of recent events Jaguar was a better name. Industry adopted the adage 'manufacture or die'. In 1948 the first postwar Motor Show saw the Morris Minor, the Jaguar XK120 and Land Rover, and the Jaguar led to

It was Bentley who first showed British cars were an international force in motor racing - by dominating Le Mans, above. Ford moved into Britain in force in 1911, left

The story of the British motor industry has been full of strange episodes and De Lorean's ill-fated venture was certainly one of them

another line of British Le Mans winners in the 1950s. Giants Austin and Morris merged in 1952 to form the British Motor Corporation - later to suck in others such as Jaguar and Daimler to form (in rapid succession) British Motor Holdings, the British Leyland Motor Corporation and, eventually, the Rover Group.

Great cars and great names have come and gone. The Suez crisis of 1956 and 1957 made the cleverly compact Mini look nicely timed in 1959, alongside the simpler Ford Anglia and Triumph Herald. The Hillman Imp followed in 1963; the Great Train Robbers struck just before Dr Beeching's Axe; and the Rover 2000 became European Car of the Year, suggesting that Rover wasn't quite as dowdy as some people thought. And in the 1960s again, Britain began to dominate Grand Prix racing.

1965 saw a 'temporary' 70mph speed limit; the 1973 Arab-Israeli war brought petrol queues and a 50mph limit. Imports had risen to 33 per cent by 1975. The government propped up British Leyland through strike and stagnation until Honda rescued it in 1980 and made it healthy enough for BMW to buy in 1994. Ford acquired both Jaguar and Aston Martin; MG has risen again; the Range Rover's star has never waned but the DeLorean and the Sinclair C5 came and went.

Now Nissan, Peugeot, Toyota and Honda all build cars in Britain. With Ford, Vauxhall, Rolls-Royce, and a uniquely British network of specialists like Lotus, Morgan and TVR, they are the heart of an industry beginning its second century. An industry largely controlled from afar, but a motor industry whose centenary truly deserves its celebration.

Gabriel Voisin's last car was just as bizarre as most of his earlier creations. Power for the Biscuter came from a tiny 125cc engine

When American designer Virgil Exner got hold of one of the last Bugatti 101 chassis this was the result, left. Pegasos were as offbeat as anything from Voisin, this Z102, below, more strange than most

PARIS RETROMOBILE 9-18 *February*

At the end of the day there were rumblings that this year's Retromobile was not one of the best, but such things are strictly relative. If you go to the great Paris show in February you can virtually guarantee that you will see things you have never seen before - and this year was no exception.

As ever, it was a show of extremes. Gabriel Voisin's creations, for example, were bizarre to the last, and the tiny alloy Biscuter at Retromobile provided living proof. Some 18,000 of them were built for the Spanish market in the 1950s, and with nothing more potent than a 125cc Gnome & Rhone two-stroke engine under the angular bodywork, they were pathetically slow. But the Biscuter had four wheels where its bubble car rivals scuttled around on three, and with front-wheel drive and a transverse engine you could almost call it modern. . .

At the other extreme were the cars from the Blackhawk collection, including that icon of late 1940s eccentricity, the Tucker; and, even more fascinating, the Virgil Exner styled Bugatti 101C - built on one of the very last Bugatti chassis. That was displayed alongside Chrysler's more recent homage to the Bugatti Atlantic, a wonderful pastiche which even Chrysler hasn't quite brought itself to put into limited production, even though the Prowler hot rod has now become reality.

And if these cars didn't satisfy the craving for something different, the contents of one hall on the fringes of the show certainly would. There stood the Le Mans Pegaso Z102 - the car which had been withdrawn from the 1953 24 Hours after its sister car had crashed in practice and killed its driver. It might have been very different; the quad cam V8 had made the Pegaso as fast as anything on the track that year. Ah, if only.

The descent into Monte Carlo, left, with only a dusting of snow to make the hairpins more treacherous for tired crews

John Buffum triumphed over almost white-out conditions to finish third overall in his Porsche 356, left. If you were wearing these, below, you would have wanted the heated version this year. . .

4-9 FEBRUARY
Monte Carlo Challenge

Retro ralliers are a tough and masochistic breed, so they suffer great torments from the middle of November on, when LE JOG has ended. Once they have recovered from the strains of taking the longest way imaginable from Lands End to John O'Groats they are faced with a barren couple of months before the next big test, and they don't come much bigger than the Monte Carlo Challenge in early February.

It's a challenge that some take perhaps too seriously. This year Kjell Gudim and Arild Antonsen fell foul of the organisers. Their Volvo Amazon had run very well. . . too well. Their illegal limited-slip diff was rumbled and they were out. Maurizio Selci didn't think it unreasonable to put a Citroen ID19 engine in his Traction Avant, either, but the powers that be thought otherwise. It's easy to see how such over enthusiasm comes about. The route is long and demanding and the weather quite likely to be appalling, so the crews need every edge they can get.

This year the weather was indeed dreadful and the cars had to contend with blizzard conditions, slippery snow and black ice. If that wasn't enough there was rain cold enough to turn to hail, and freezing fog to make the cocktail complete. At least the weather was democratic. It waited until the cars had all congregated at Colmar in eastern France before becoming really awful.

A record number of cars started this year's event - 161 in all covering 19 different nationalities and from four different start points, in Bristol, Oslo, St Moritz and Noordwijk in the Netherlands. It was a high quality entry too for this, the seventh running of the Challenge, topped by three-times winner Ron Gammons, partnered in his 1962 MGA by Jane Bourne as a last

Whoever packed this shovel on their luggage carrier, left, probably had a fairly good idea of what they were letting themselves in for. Equipping your MGB with chains on the rear wheels helps give you the edge on MG drivers lacking such forethought

minute recruit for the seat normally occupied by Paul Easter. They were up against another former winner in the guise of Nicky Porter (with Andrew Bodman in a Mercedes 220SE) and famous names ranging from American rally champion John Buffum (partnering Neil Wilson in his Porsche 356) to Liberal MP and Monte Carlo Challenge regular Sir David Steel in his 1961 Riley 1.5. The record entry also included twenty teams in the pre 1949 category, the oldest of which was a 1910 La France, driven by Edi Schomo and Roman Schlommer, starting from St Moritz and relying on rear brakes only.

It was the organisers' intention to recreate the Monte format of the early days 'when production cars driven by true amateurs overcame the challenge of snow-covered Alpine passes'. After the cars had all gathered in Place Rapp in Colmar from their various starting points it was onto the Alps and into the blizzards straight from Siberia. Endurance then took over from speed and low slung sports cars had to give best to saloons, and big saloons at that. Big saloons have full weather protection, reasonable comfort and efficient heaters - imagine some of the oldest runners without so much as roof or windscreen, driver and navigator wrapped in flying jackets or whatever but still out in the bitter cold. Strongly fancied runners like previous winners Ron Gammons in his MGA had their cars defeated by the conditions. The Mercedes, though, were in their element - just as they had been back in 1960 when the real Monte was held in similiarly dire conditions and the big German cars won. Then it was a big budget team managed by Karl Kling, run along the same ultra competitive lines as the racing team that had recently been disbanded. Those cars had started from Warsaw and finished 1-2-3, led by Walter Schock and Rolf Moll on their way to the 1960 European Rally Championship.

The drivers in 1996 had too much on their minds to hark back to those days, but come Monte Carlo it was again two Mercedes first and second. Winners were the Scandinavian trio of Monty Karlan, Ake Gustavsson and Torhild Halle but their surprisingly agile Merc 220SE had the slightest of leads, just four seconds, ahead of another 220SE, that of Ignacio Sunsundegui from Spain and Britain's Colin Francis. Navigator Francis was delighted and not surprisingly declared that this year's event, the seventh Monte Carlo Challenge, was the best ever.

The two Mercedes had finished ahead of a far more recognised rally pairing, in a Porsche 356, John Buffum, accustomed to winning the American championship in years gone by, and Neil Wilson, himself a winner in the RAC. The same car and crew had come second last year but they were still very happy to finish so high in such conditions. Previous winners Nicky Porter and Andrew Bodman (who had finished fifth last year), could well have repeated their win had they not slid off the road on the ice not far from home, losing enough time to drop their Mercedes 220SE down to sixth. A shame that because otherwise the Mercedes team would have had the perfect repeat of that 1960 triumph. Their car should know the way to Monte Carlo by now as it's one of the very few to have competed in all seven events, and with the same crew. Fourth place had gone to the Corns/Cave Volvo 122S with fifth going to the Scharowski/Scharowski and Allmen Citroen ID19, with a team of three to share the load.

The Grand Touring class was won by the 1937 Delahaye driven by Burchardt/Schnellman ahead of another 1937 car, the Alvis of William/Davis while, proving that a blower Bentley can last the pace, one finished third. W.O. would have been surprised. By the finish over fifty of the 161 cars had run out of the allotted time and not suprisingly none of the finishers had avoided collecting penalty points, the totals of some of those at the tail of the field being of truly astronomical proportions.

On the level, with the snow cleared, the conditions were not a problem but very little of the rally fell into that desirable category - as this Dutch Healey was later to discover

The MG Magnette shows its battle scars on the rear door, and would you like to have been the person getting back into that Bentley in the morning?

Peter Deckers' and Luc Hendrickx's 1962 Austin Healey MkII equipped with studded tyres for extra grip, right. MG Magnettes, opposite page, may not win you an event but they will get you to the finish

GALWAY RALLY 16-18 February

If it's wet, if there's an Atlantic breeze trying to bowl you over, if you're stuck in a horrendous traffic jam, and if it's February - you must be in Galway. Although the entry lists in the Irish Historic Tarmac series may be smaller than some of those in the rest of Europe, the lure of closed public road stages guarantees a strong influx from the UK mainland. Porsches are currently the cars to beat in historic rallying and Maidstone's Geoff Crabtree had his mint green example at number one, closely followed by former tarmac champion John Coyne, with Martin Dolan. Then there was John Keatley from Magherafelt, partnered by Maurice Beckett followed by 911 number four, the yellow car of Dessie Nutt and Derek Smyth. The rest of the field offered the variety of everything from Lotus Cortina and BMW 2002Tii to Lancia Fulvia and TR4 - not forgetting the inevitable rash of Cooper Ss.

The Galway Motor Club had contrived a 122-mile route on which former champion John Coyne, only recently persuaded out of retirement, set a blistering pace ahead of Englishman Geoff Crabtree while behind him, having only recently joined the Stuttgart steamrollers, Dessie Nutt was on a steep learning curve

By the time the rally left Galway on Sunday no-one was expecting anything other than a Porsche win: the only question, with Crabtree pushing Coyne as hard as he could while still watching his own mirrors for a charging Keatley, was which one.

In the end it turned out to be John Coyne who maintained the steadiest progress on roads literally awash with standing water to take a well deserved win - but it was 1995 Demon Tweeks/Classic and Sportscar champion John Keatley who sneaked into second on the penultimate stage when Crabtree and Jordan slid off the road and into retirement. Behind them, Dessie Nutt christened his new Porsche with a fine third place, the Lancia boys took fourth, and Alan Courtney's Cortina carried the scars of its contact with a wall to an honourable fifth.

John Keatley and Maurice Beckett took their 911 up into second place during the penultimate stage and stayed there until the finish

Without a 911 you're at a dis-advantage in this series, but David and Robin Hollis still brought their BMW 2002Tii home in a respectable seventh place, right. Geoff Crabtree's 911, below, retired after crashing

Like most people on the Pomeroy, Chloe Mason was getting in useful practice for the coming season. It would pay off as she would later win at the St John Horsfall meeting in June

What constitutes a good touring car? In the Pomeroy scheme of things certainly not the Collins' Lamborghini Urraco, left. It's Silverstone in February, so of course it's cold and wet, not that the TRs mind, below

POMEROY TROPHY 24 February

If cricket is a mystery to other Europeans, with the honourable exception of the Dutch, what they would make of the annual Pomeroy Trophy is anyone's guess. Its rules are far more complicated even than cricket's. In theory the object of the exercise is to find the finest touring car among the invariably arcane collection which turns up at the Silverstone circuit each February. Thus Edwardian monsters such as the 1911 Knox can be seen mixing it with cars generations apart, such as Tony Moy's London to Mexico Escort (an eventual 14th), Bruce Spollon's 1932 Alfa and another old rally star in the shape of the Chevette 2300HS of Andy Johnson (which finally took tenth).

It must be a strange formula indeed when a chain-gang Frazer Nash can win, so perhaps this was just a freak one-off result? Not at all, two more Nashes were second and third. 'Touring car' implies some degree of comfort but winner James Baxter spent the days before the event in fabricating the required roof frame for his car out of conduit. He could have driven his other car, a TVR 3000M, but the rules favour older, small-engined cars. They do so to such a degree that a touring car in the grandest possible fashion in the shape of the Lamborghini Espada was out of it, as was its cousin the Urraco.

There are five events in all, including a high-speed slalom around a line of cones to assess steering performance. Then comes a braking test (not the Knox's forte) and an acceleration test which showed the Frazer Nashes in a good light even compared with modern cars like Porsches. The test usually enjoyed most is the forty-minute race - and so it was this year, despite the fact that this time torrential rain was combined with stiff cross winds and enough water on the track to make aquaplaning all too easy.

In the end it never really matters; for most of those imvolved, the Pomeroy Trophy is just the first opportunity to get a car on the track while winter is still present. And that's enough.

The Grande Réserve of Cigars.

Some of life's great pleasures require both time and skill in their making.

The Dunhill Aged Cigar is one such example, a fine spirit such as Cognac another.

From manufacture to the appreciation of the intrinsic qualities of each, the Dunhill Aged Cigar and the finest Cognacs have much in common.

Both have roots in the soil culminating in the harvest of tobacco leaf or grape.

Both require the attentions of a Master Blender to ensure the end result consistently yields the highest standards of quality.

And both are aged and matured in wood to impart their unique and individual character.

A smoothness and mellowness of taste is also common to both, as is a subtlety of aroma.

Perhaps that's why, enjoyed together, they provide a perfect partnership.

And why the Dunhill Aged Cigar deserves to share Cognac's highest appellation – The Grande Réserve of Cigars.

The Frazer Nashes were in fine form, winning the Pom and also coming second. This is the Pilkington car, ahead of King's 1936 Talbot and Malyan's 1939 BMW 328

Some cars were just never intended to have hoods. Their designers intended that drivers should be stoic enough to drive them open - but the Pomeroy Trophy regulations do dictate that hoods are used

RALLYE DU MAROC 23-30 *March*

It was somehow appropriate that an Alpine A110 won the third Rallye du Maroc classic, with French crews taking five out of the first six places, but it wasn't a straight-run thing. In the end, the French Alpine duo of Stephane Roux and Vincent Repoux finished well clear of a tight battle for second place, and that in turn was finally resolved in favour of the Consten/Consten E-type with the Bessade/Bessade Aston Martin DB2/4 in third place ahead of Belgians Dehaeck and Heite in their Ferrari 365 GTB/4.

But fourth place must have been a disappointment for the Belgian Ferrari crew, as they were actually looking to be quite comfortably in command until the cars came to the wonderfully named Tizi'n'Test col, and over its 2092 metres things changed dramatically, with Roux and Repoux taking over in a lead they were never to lose over the rest of the week.

Compared with the previous two Rallye du Maroc Classics the 1600km route was 80 per cent the same as before, and all on tarmac but this time bringing the crews further west and within sight of the Atlantic. Day one started with a short familiarisation stage to help drivers get accustomed to African conditions, traffic and to the route book, taking the cars through narrow roads and small villages. The real business started the next evening with the Grand Prix of Casablanca-Ain Sebaa, run on a circuit on the outskirts of Casablanca, through the walled district of Ain Sebaa.

And maybe you can't go too far wrong on a circuit, but the next day presented navigators with their first test - and one where, as the briefing resignedly put it, 'the road book will not help, the road signs are either absent or at best in Arabic and the map does not always agree with the road. . .'

The reward for getting through that was to enjoy the fast stretch sweeping through the Atlantic dunes on the way to Mogador - where the Ferraris of the Rinaldi and Seydoux teams, a Boxer and a 250GT, were in their element. By Wednesday the crews had been through Agadir and Taroudannt and over the Sous Valley and were ready for some serious driving. That came at the 'Road to the Clouds' stage, which was once part of the World Rally Championship route.

As the name suggest it climbs steeply, to 2200 metres with dozens of hairpin bends and a long way to drop. In a superb display the Belgian pair of Chalot and Derecque hurled their heavy XK150 up first, ahead of far more suitable machinery, in particular the A110 of the eventual winners Roux/Repoux.

Next it was on to an overnight stop in Marrakesh before another classic stage over the mountains up to the biggest dam in Morocco, at Bin el Ouidane. The stage around the lake was won by the Seydoux/Seydoux Ferrari 250 GT team without dropping a point, ahead of the Lancia Stratos of Mattei/Mattei. Just as impressive was the performance of Fenouil/Puce who took their big Lincoln Pan Americana to fifth on that stage - an unlikely looking car proving more agile than it looked.

By the end of Stage 5 Roux and Repoux in the Alpine A110 were firmly in charge, well over 100 points clear of the Bessades' Aston, and they were proving to be consistency itself, usually right at the top at each stage.

The rally culminated on the Friday with the Marrakesh Grand Prix, the second circuit event. In a nice touch this was open to all the cars which had already retired and threw up new winners, the Springers in their Lancia Aurelia, but close behind once more was that A110. It had been a good week for them.

Once the rapid Alpine A110 of Stephane Roux and Vincent Repoux had taken the lead, at Tizi'n'Test, they stayed there until the finish in Marrakesh

The winning Alpine A110 finished ahead of the Jaguar E-type of Bernard Consten and his son, and the Bessades' Aston Martin DB2/4

The Atlas Mountains provided the backdrop for much of the rally, centre. d'El Kholti's Iso Rivolta, left, stormed through the Tizi'n'Test section

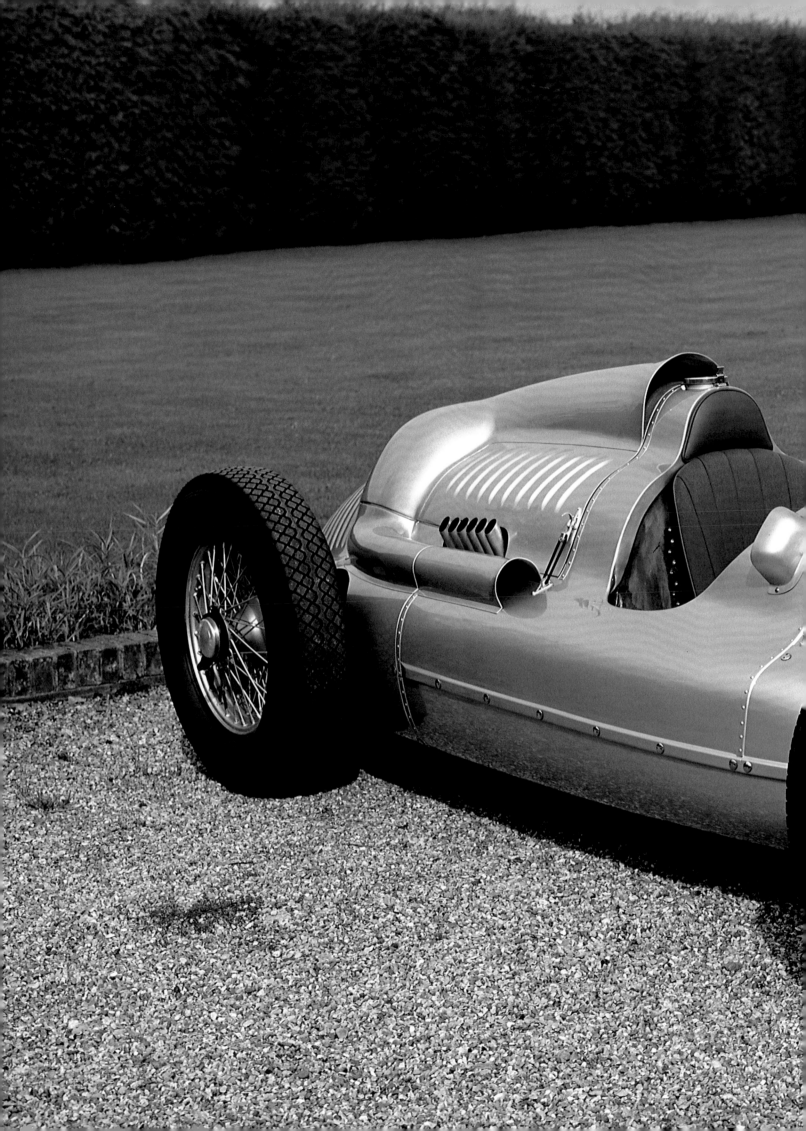

Original Sins?

*Racing cars, by their very nature, do not stay the same for long.
They are developed, they are broken and repaired, they move on.
KEVIN BRAZENDALE asks how original is original,
when so much may have been changed?*

Martin Stretton in what used to be the Plate Special but is now restored to former glory as a 'real' Talbot. Is that wrong?

A couple of years ago, one of Britain's best known restorers finished work on the oldest Grand Prix Ferrari. It had taken Tony Merrick five years to undo the ravages of time and worse. But by the time he'd finished, the V12 166 F2 car was as good as new. And whatever the nuts and bolts, so to speak, of the restoration project, no one could seriously object to such an historic car being rescued. Or could they?

Well, some do; and they are the ones who will argue that this Ferrari as it now stands, resplendent in its blue and yellow Argentine racing colours, is in no sense 'genuine'. Yet look at its history. Colin Crabbe discovered it in Argentina back in 1978 - in such poor condition that it was more than ten years before a saviour came forward with sufficient funds for what was always going to be a long, demanding and expensive restoration. Merrick was then handed a chassis which had been chopped about and widened to take a Chrysler V8 when the complex 1.5-litre Ferrari V12 had given up the ghost - plus what amounted to a big box of bits with most of the suspension and some of the original engine. In his subsequent rebuild, Merrick used as many of the original parts as possible, but still had to make (or have made) a huge number of missing or unusable components, often working from old photographs as the original drawings no longer exist. And Shapecraft had to make a new body, working on the same basis.

So the end result is brilliant and usable - but is it, in the strict sense, a genuine, original car? And here is where we come to matters of definition. Genuine? Well, yes; because no one disputes that Crabbe found an old Ferrari. But original, once Tony Merrick had finished with it? Obviously not; how could it be?

Or what of the two Auto Unions that Paul and Barbara Karassik extracted from the Soviet Union some years ago. More accurately, what the Karassiks acquired was the potential for two cars; in practice the bits had to go to restorers Crosthwaite & Gardner to be turned into one D-type V12 of 1938 spec, and one of 1939 spec. Even some of the parts which were original and apparently in good order, like the cylinder heads, had to be recast.

Into those heads went new valves and new springs. Below them ran new pistons in new liners; and so it went on. The silver bodies were a masterpiece of alloy shaping by Rod Jolley, and the end results were a joy to all who saw and heard them. But once again, you would be hard pushed to call the cars original.

Does it really matter? Surely only a real pedant would argue that the historically important Ferrari and neglected Auto Unions should have been left as found, and that in some way their restoration actually devalues those old cars which have continuous histories and which you can still see circulating in historic racing.

Competition Delahaye 135 is the French equivalent of Bentley - saloons can frequently turn into racers

Maybe it matters most in cases where the end result is so desirable that it would be almost criminal not to do the work. Below that category though is a far greyer area.

Recently Sean Danaher finished a fine restoration of a 1927 Grand Prix Talbot; but look closely at what he had to work with. What he acquired was more like a 159 Alfetta than any Talbot; yet Talbot it was. An Italian enthusiast had owned it in the late 1940s, had a new tubular chassis made, and clothed it in a pretty, Alfa-like body. With original Talbot running gear and engine, however, the Plate Special (as it was known) was uncompetitive, faded into retirement and stayed there until David Cohen acquired it and decided to have it turned it back into a Talbot.

Now in many ways, it needed less major work than the Ferrari 166 that we started this discussion with. The engine was very complete, the only major thing it required was new connecting rods. The body and chassis had to go, of course, and exacting replicas were made of the originals, again often working from old photographs and contemporary magazine features rather than from drawings, which had long since disappeared. Old photographs also indicated that the instruments in the Special were the original Talbot's so could be reused.

The result is a masterpiece; but around half the car is now new, and an existing car (albeit one of no great historical importance) was destroyed to build it.

So was the project justifiable? Again the answer must be yes. The Talbots were incredible GP cars with complex twin-cam, straight-eight, roller-bearing engines. They were overshadowed by one of the greatest of all GP cars, the 1.5-litre straight-eight Delage, but once the works team had given up on them they were eventually sorted out to become very competitive. Simply to see one in action again, as a pointer to just what might have been, would surely be worth the loss of the virtually unknown and certainly unsuccessful Plate Special. . ?

A different case is the creation of car from a disparate collection of genuine parts - one recently restored 1929 Bugatti Type 44 providing a perfect example.

Seven years ago, a genuine chassis (with numbers and history), was found in a scrapyard, and the modifications it had been subjected to reversed. An engine, itself little more than scrap and in need of a total rebuild, came from Barry Price. And a Type 44 Vanvooren body, once used for target practice by the German army, was found in Holland. The end result, depending on your point of view, is either that a rare Bugatti saloon lives again, or that a new Bugatti has been born. The grey is getting greyer.

So how much do you need to build a genuine car from its ashes (sometimes literally)? Just the chassis plate is enough for some, but what is really required? A chassis? A chassis and an engine? You could argue until the cows come home.

Money talks, too. Only a few years ago, when speculative money had got really out of hand, the courts deemed that Bentley

Several GP Auto Unions, as above left, were hidden away during the war. Paul and Barbara Karassik retrieved two V12 D-Types from Russia. To return them to a viable state implied a total rebuild. What is the alternative?

Recreations of valuable road cars are as much of a dilemma as the racing equivalent. Eric Koux's 'new' Bugatti Atlantic is a perfect replica but doesn't claim to be anything else

'Old Number One' was the real thing - when little more than its main bulkhead had actually played any part in winning Le Mans in 1929. But that is perhaps the most extreme case of them all, such anomalies are rare, and in Britain, at least, the VSCC has a very sensible approach to such problems.

'Postwar cars', according to the Club's philosophy, 'have to have a continuous history; but before that we like to see original cars. The rules do allow for cars made from genuine bits, although we don't encourage copies. We apply a very simple rule of thumb in considering a car. We divide it into five major parts and the car has to have three from the original period to be considered - while the construction also has to be in the manner of the period'.

Those five major parts are the chassis frame, front axle, rear axle, engine casing and gearbox casing. Why only the casings? Well it gets involved stripping engines to try and verify parts, and in any case, in competition cars in particular, engine internals get changed over the years in inevitable rebuilds and repairs.

Within those guidelines, 'new' old cars are still being produced and the VSCC will quite happily discuss what's being done as the car progresses, 'a sort of outline planning permission if you like' as the VSCC puts it, to save the enthusiast building a complete car only to have the club unwilling to accept its provenance.

This approach dates only from 1989 and owes something to the success gained by Ivan Dutton, racing a Bugatti Type 35 with many new parts. Some with more original cars complained; but as Dutton puts it, 'They couldn't do too much, because Mayman was going round in a totally new ERA (AJM1), so this five-part rule was thought up'.

And while agreeing that the rule makes sense (and currently competing in a Type 35 with original front axle, back axle and gearbox, for three out of five) Dutton offers an interesting slant: 'One thing it does do', he says, 'with Bugattis at any rate, is to make some of those five components worth far too much. With something like, say, a Riley there are masses of parts around and so very few problems. But with a Bugatti, spares which might normally be fitted to an original car are potentially the basis for a whole new car - and as such they're worth far more'.

The VSCC's attitudes are sensible. They are concerned that people know what they are looking at and that there is no attempt to pass things off as what they are not. The ERA mentioned by Ivan Dutton is a good example. It is known as AJM1 rather than R15b to indicate that it was made up from parts - genuine ERA parts it's true, but it never existed as a contemporary ERA. It was assembled by Anthony James Merrick (hence the AJM) using a good 80 per cent ERA content, but it isn't a 'genuine' ERA.

And while the ERA ranks have only grown by one, 250F Maseratis are still breeding - although that's not a source of great concern to the VSCC either. 'Cameron Millar produces 250Fs, but they all have his chassis number, from CM1 up to CM10 and everyone knows what they are getting. Up to CM8 they were all pretty well original parts, so we accept those; beyond that there are more manufactured parts involved'.

These days more and more cars can be assembled from remanufactured spares. Bugattis are a prime example but the Bugatti Owners Club has a good idea of what's original and what's not; and as the VSCC points out, 'the grapevine is very good; people remember cars and what happened to them, they hear of people remanufacturing batches of parts and are alert to the possibility of new cars appearing'.

Another source of debate is when a production model, and a perfectly good car in its own right, is butchered to make something more exotic. Prime candidates for the chop have long been those Bentley saloons sacrificed to make Le Mans replicas. These days you might be forgiven for thinking the only cars Bentley made between the wars were the archetypal Vanden Plas bodied Le Mans cars, because so many of the saloons have gone. Granted the saloons were very often the staider end of 1930s British coach-

Ivan Dutton's success with extensively rebuilt Bugatti T35 helped prompt 'five-part' rule. This T35 in jigsaw form meets the criterion of three or more out of five original units as defined by the VSCC rules

building, and unlikely to set the blood racing; but did they deserve to die for that? Many Alfas go the same way too, as there were some remarkably conservative bodies on Alfa chassis just crying out, in some buyers' eyes, to be turned into open Zagato or Touring replicas.

Just occasionally it's not the dull looking cars that suffer. The 1933 8C2300 Alfa auctioned at Brooks in 1995 had a striking aerodynamic Viotti coupe body, like a smaller version of the fabulous factory 8C2900 coupes; but its new owner planned to dispense with that and turn it back into the Le Mans model it once was. Is that the restoration of an Alfa back to a historically significant model, or the wanton destruction of a car that had its own strong identity?

You can argue both sides of the case. True, this car did finish third at Le Mans in 1933; but the 'new' coupe body had been on the car since 1935. So will the restored car be more original than the coupe? Hardly. But as the owner, you pays your money and takes your choice. The saving grace here is that the aero body was not destroyed and should find its way onto another chassis.

In defence of the butchers you can point to Specials like any of the aero-engined monsters that appeared in the 1920s - or perhaps to Mother Gun, a genuine Le Mans Bentley turned in the 1930s into the Jackson Special, the silver record breaker which Stanley Mann campaigns today. No-one now says what a criminal thing that was to have done to the original car. But that's a special case and really too strong a defence. The problem with manufac-

turing Le Mans type Bentleys on genuine chassis is twofold, the destruction of existing cars and the devaluing of the real thing.

Britain was not alone in this, Delahayes went the same way in France because the Competition 135 was so much more desirable than the saloons on the same chassis - and the bodies were easy enough to recreate. After a while there were far more Competition 135s around than ever left the factory.

At the end of the day, the real problem is deception. When the object of the exercise is not just to produce another homage to an acknowledged classic (something which, for instance, has seen the Dane Eric Koux produce the most perfect Bugatti Atlantic replicas imaginable), but to deceive - which is what a number of the Delahaye builders were guilty of. Then, not only is the car modified but so is its provenance. Cars long since destroyed are discovered and revived. Ironically such a car might have just as much original content as a perfectly genuine restoration, as in the case of the infamous Ferrari scam uncovered in Italy three years ago. The fake Testa Rossa and 250LM then uncovered among others were the work of the sort of craftsmen who built the originals; and with Ferrari themselves supplying many of the parts the end results were naturally very impressive.

Perhaps the product might have been nearly as good as the original, but the matter had gone far beyond the sometimes petty questions of what is and is not genuine. This was outright fraud fuelled by the huge prices that only the real thing commands. In this case at least, grey had turned starkly to black and white.

1938 Viotti bodied Alfa 8C2300 was formerly a Le Mans model and will be turned back into one. The good news in this case is that the lovely coupe body will not be destroyed

Cartier

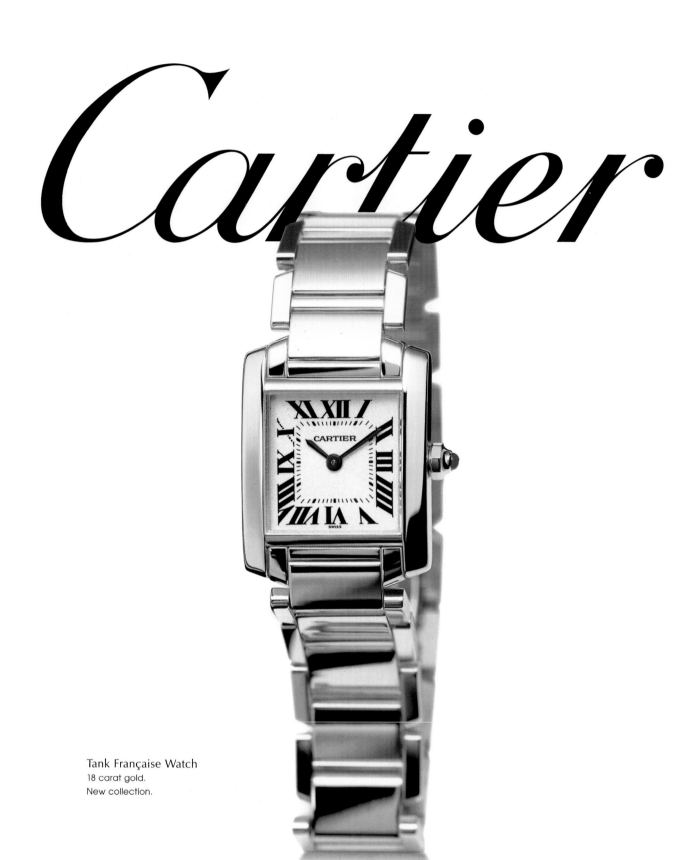

Tank Française Watch
18 carat gold.
New collection.

THE ART OF BEING UNIQUE

Cartier, 175/176 New Bond Street, London W1, Telephone: 0171-493 6962, 188 Sloane Street, London SW1, Telephone: 0171-235 9023, The Fine Jewellery Room and The International Room of Luxury at Harrods, Telephone: 0171-730 1234, Heathrow Terminal 4, Telephone: 0181-745 6724 and leading jewellers throughout the United Kingdom and Ireland. For information on your nearest stockist please call 0171-493 6962.

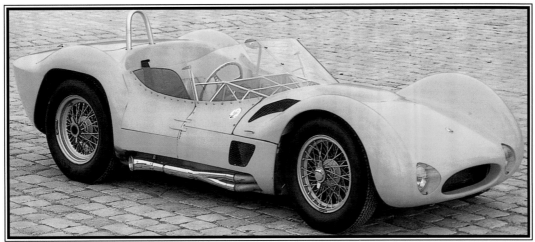

Bidding on the ex-Jim Hall, ex-Carroll Shelby Maserati Birdcage set the early season running for classic racer prices

SPRING

With the sporting season starting to get into its stride, and British motor industry centenary events in particular starting to spice up the calendar, Spring held a number of treats for the enthusiast. For those with deep pockets there were some famous cars in the sales. For those with even bigger ambitions, there was even a famous marque. . .

13-14 April
While classic enthusiasts celebrated with the Lotus Festival at Donington Park, the uncertainty over the future of the financially beleaguered company dragged on, with real doubts surfacing again over whether the troubled marque was likely to survive at all in the longer term.

20 April
A 1934-35 7.1-litre supercharged Mercedes SSK two-seat competition spyder, once owned by Adrian and Denis Conan Doyle, the sons of Sir Arthur Conan Doyle, was a star of the Brooks' sale at the Daimler-Benz Museum in Stuttgart. It was described as 'ready to run, ready to race'.

27-28 April
In the way that only American auto enthusiasts can, Edwards Air Force Base (previously known as the Muroc desert) hosted a hot-rodders reunion in co-operation with the Southern California Timing Association - one of the organisations that brought drag racing in from the streets in the late 1940s and early 1950s, and sanctioned the dry-lake record runs that America became famous for.

27-28 April
Beetle fans flock to the 'Gran Concentracion de Escarabajos en Las Islas Baleares'. Escarabajos, if you hadn't made the connection, is the Spanish for beetles.

4-6 May
The Classic and Sportscar Show and Auto Windscreens Century of Motoring celebration at the NEC, Birmingham, offered an interesting way of selling your classic car - or perhaps shopping for one. For £30 a day or £60 for three days you could display your vehicle in what was described as a 'Live Classified' car park. Better than browsing through all those grainy pictures and imaginative descriptions.

15 May
Brooks sold a 1960/61 Maserati Tipo 61 Birdcage for £464,834 at their Monaco sale - the highest auction price paid for a classic racer so far this year. Meanwhile, model maker Paul's Model Art is reported to have done a deal with McLaren to produce an amazing series of models, in various scales, which will include every McLaren ever made, from Bruce's Austin Seven Ulster special to the current F1 cars.

15 May
The first shipment of Aston Martin DB7s - coupes and convertibles and undoubtedly classics of the future - is being loaded up outside the Newport Pagnell factory for shipment to the USA. Success of the DB7 has made Aston more secure than of late.

16 May
Christie's sale in Geneva included a fine collection of Grand Prix drivers' helmets, collected over the years by former Lotus Grand Prix Team Manager Peter Warr. Helmets on offer included ones worn by Senna, Mansell, Piquet, Ickx, Peterson, Rosberg, Hunt and many more. Just the thing to go with one of their old F1 cars perhaps?

18 May
A plaque was unveiled on the Rhine-quay in Arnhem, commemorating the arrival, 100 years to the day earlier, of the first car in Holland - the inevitable Benz, imported from Germany.

29 May
Now the rumour is that former Fl driver Brian Henton is entering the bidding for the Lotus name. . .

2 June
When Michael Schumacher won the Spanish Grand Prix, it was also the fiftieth Grand Prix that Ferrari had won in partnership with fuel and oil supplier Shell. Their first win together was way back in 1951.

4 June
To celebrate the centenary of Ford's first car, a replica of the 1896 Ford Quadricycle is shown at Beaulieu. At first the car refuses to run, then having been persuade to go, it refuses to stop. In the true tradition of the father of all horseless carriages, the Cugnot steam wagon, its progress was eventually halted by ramming a wall, happily without great damage or injury. Ford also celebrated its racing heritage with a fine display of GT40s and other sporting Fords.

11 June
A plaque was unveiled by Britain's Society of Motor Manufacturers and Traders and the Royal Automobile Club to the memory of Frederick Simms, who founded what became the RAC in 1897, and the SMMT in 1902. Simms is known as the father of the British motor industry, having imported the first Daimler to the UK in 1893, before selling the rights to Henry Lawson. The plaque is on a railway arch near Putney Bridge in London, on the site of one of Simms' first workshops.

15 June
An incredible convoy of thirty D-type and XKSS Jaguars had driven from Coventry to Le Mans to celebrate the fortieth anniversary of the D-type's last works win in the 24-Hour classic. The collection was valued at around £14 million. Ford also celebrated it Le Mans exploits, with a restaging of its attempted GT40 dead heat.

16 June
Continuing the British motor industry's centenary celebrations, the ambitious aim of the third annual running of the Brooklands British Sports Car Day, organised by the Gordon Keeble Owners Club, is to exhibit one example of every British sportscar ever built. Where would you start. . ?

Villa d'Este

From 1932 to 1939 was a golden age of custom coachbuilding and some of the best examples of the coachbuilder's art were gathered for the concours at the Villa d'Este, on the shores of Lake Como in April

How important was the Villa d'Este concours in the 1930s and 1940s? Important enough for Alfa Romeo to name one of their models after the last of them in 1949. Since then it's only been held three times and appropriately enough, in 1996 Alfa Romeo won - with a wonderful 8C 2900B entered by the Swiss dealer Lukas Huni. Its Touring-built body was on show for the first time since its restoration by Tony Merrick.

Despite the huge appeal of the Alfa, the spectators who decide on the biggest trophy, the Coppa d'Oro, gave that to a Hooper-bodied Bentley. From the shores of Lake Como that must presumably look more exotic than the home grown Alfa.

The 1996 concours was for cars from 1932 to 1939 and the Alfa and Bentley were up against 44 other cars, the likes of the Figoni & Falaschi Goutte d'Eau Talbot-Lago SS T150C, two other Alfa 8C 2900s, one of which was once owned by Nino Farina, Nick Channing's 1939 Vanden Plas bodied V12 Lagonda and a brace of Mercedes 500Ks. One of those, the 1936 Special Roadster, was runner up to the Alfa.

Amongst the Mercedes ranks was the special streamlined Type 320 saloon from 1939, entered by the Mercedes Benz Museum in Stuttgart, but which went unrewarded by the judges. The Musee International de l'Automobile in Geneva also entered one of their cars, the Kellner bodied Hispano Suiza J12.

The Farina-owned Alfa wasn't the only car with a celebrity in its past. It was kept company by the ghost of Mussolini who once owned the 6C 2300 Touring and of Tazio Nuvolari, the erstwhile owner of the Zagato bodied 1934 8C 2300. Famous previous owners cut no ice with the judges though. They were there to judge style and that was there in abundance, particularly in the Goutte d'Eau Talbot; but the shape, sublime to some, is almost a caricature to others and the judges did not feel inclined to put it any higher than sixth, behind the sleek 1938 Pourtout-bodied Lancia Astura. They were, however, sufficiently smitten by Karl Bloechle's magnificently ugly 1936 Voisin Aerosport to give that a trophy, even if it did not place in the overall top ten. Bloechle had driven the Vosin through the snow to the show and deserved a prize for that alone when so many others trailer their cars.

It was a stunning array on the shores of Lake Como. If you admire character rather than beauty, the aerodynamic Voisins were the stars. They are seen to the right of the white Packard, above. Overall winner was the Tony Merrick restored Touring-bodied Alfa 8C 2900B, seen right. Completely over the top or the very pinnacle of 1930s style? That's the issue with the amazing Goutte d'Eau (or teardrop) Talbot Lago, on the previous page

The Safari Rally is one of those events where historics piggy-back on the modern championship version. Echoing the days when Peugeots dominated the event, David Horsey and John Lloyd won this year in their 504, having splashed through one of the wettest routes on record. The Green and Gittens Ford Comet rose above most of the problems

The Sean Treacy Lancia Fulvia couldn't emulate its fourth place on the Galway Historic and was never in the running

The David and Gary Moore Imp, left, was beautifully prepared but was soon out with mechanical failure. The flying progress of Dessie Nutt's Porsche 911, below, ended with a broken driveshaft

CIRCUIT OF IRELAND 5-8 *April*

As befits any event with the history and allure of the Circuit of Ireland, 1996 saw the largest entry of any historic stage rally ever held in Ireland. Much interest centered on former World Ladies Rally Champion Louise Aitken Walker and former European Historic Champion Hendrik Blok in Porsche 911s.

Aitken Walker was in the white Tuthill-prepared Porsche into which owner Dr Betty Crawford has previously persuaded such notables as Walter Rohrl, Stig Blomqvist and Jimmy McRae. Hendrik Blok brought his 911 to taste the unique challenge of rallying on Irish roads.

From the North Down start in Bangor, the crowds thronged the stages, as excellent weather encouraged thousands of spectators. Publicity was so good that the famous Sally Cap stage just south of Dublin saw in excess of 30,000 rally fans, so that with few access roads and marshalls a reluctant decision was made to abandon the stage on safety grounds.

Stage 2, Hamilton's Folly, claimed the number one seed, Louise Aitken Walker. The Porsche landed heavily on one of the stage's famous jumps and its gearbox casing sheared in two. Despite the efforts of the Classic Tuthill entourage, the Scottish Shepherdess was soon back on the ferry for Duns in Scotland.

If Frank Tuthill had been blessed with the gift of clairvoyance he might even have joined her, as this was to be the weekend on which the Porsche bubble almost burst. Coyne, Keatley and Crabtree in their 911s continued where they had left off in Galway; Dessie Nutt was also in blistering form.

Although the Porsche steamroller appeared to be continuing, with Coyne and Crabtree trading seconds per stage, about this time question marks on the famed reliability of the German cars started. Dessie Nutt's car broke a driveshaft and retired. Hendrik Blok's machine started to lose power, and although he lasted into day two, the air-cooled flat-six cried enough on the

Sunday run north. John Coyne's 911 then parted company with its gearbox on stage 20 and more than a few punters started wondering whether it was possible that Porsche's day of reckoning was nigh. However such a pace was set at the front that the surviving 911s of Crabtree and Keatley had a respectable cushion to fall back on if they had problems.

On his debut event in Ireland with a new car, Drew Wylie, partnered by Neil Ewing, was proving to be the only contender even close to 911 pace. Their red Lotus Elan had proved quick on the bumpy tarmac and despite many thinking that it would be too fragile to last, a strong third place seemed to be on the cards.

So as the crews reached Bangor on Sunday evening all eyes were back on the two 911s at the head of the field. And quite what rest Francis Tuthill had on that night we will never know, but the final run on Monday was about to test his servicing skills to the limit. Crabtree broke a suspension mounting and dropped time and just when it looked as though Keatley could smell victory, his white machine went onto three cylinders and retirement seemed assured.

At the Ballymeena service stop, the Porsche crews seemed more worried than any number of the other competitors, but a well judged piece of welding saved the Crabtree car and after some nail biting he took victory. 'St Francis' had laid his hands on Keatley's engine and cured the sick animal; and to say John Keatley was grateful would have been an understatement - it was a fine 2nd place.

The Tuthill team had saved the day again but one wonders at what expense to Francis Tuthill's nerves. One wag was heard to say that the famous wide-brimmed hat that Mr T likes to wear was only there to stop him pulling out what remains of his hair.

It had been a fine event with glorious weather, a terrific entry and peerless organisation. The Lotus Elan led home the rest, with Lotus Cortinas fourth and fifth.

Many of the Circuit's stages are designed with perfect opportunities to see the cars, like this Firenza, fly through the air

Robert McGimpsey's MGB, right, came home a fine sixth behind two Lotus Cortinas. One-time European rally champion Hendrick Blok's 911, below, was another Porsche to retire

In 1959, Jaguar had a dream ...

... in 1995, we have made it come true.

The MK2. In 1959, Jaguar Cars Ltd. designed an all-time classic.
In 1995, we have brought it close to perfection. With state of the art technology, comfort and safety.
People say that the quality of our MK2 4.2 Injection equals that of the world's best limousines.
We invite you to put it to the test. Personally.

Roadster Group

TULPENRALLYE 16-20 April

If you accumulate just ninety penalty points in the course of 2200km of driving, through four countries in five days, you deserve to win; and that's exactly what the Belgian pairing of Roger Munda and Robert Roriffe achieved in the Tulpenrallye. It was a fine result for Belgium as they had a mere six crews in the field of nearly two hundred.

Their yellow Porsche 911 finished ahead of Eddy van den Hoorn and Rene Smeets, who could not repeat last year's victory in their Volvo 122S, with Linus Verhoek's Austin Healey 3000 in third and an impressive fourth place going to Constantius Steger's Jaguar XK120, one place better than his fighting fifth in this event the previous year.

The Tulpenrallye has now been held 43 times, and Maurice Gatsonides, now unfortunately better known for inventing the Gatso camera than for his rallying exploits, has figured in nine of them, having helped set up the event in 1949. In 1996 at the age of 85 he was given the honour of starting with car no 1 as this was to be his final competitive appearance in a career highlighted by his 1953 Monte Carlo win. Gatsonides had never won the Tulpenrallye and hoped that driving a replica of his 1953 winning Ford Zephyr would change his luck. At least his co-driver, 70-year old Bob Dichout, was a previous winner, so perhaps that would help too. Dichout's win had come in 1983 and he was notching up his 13th appearance. In reality of course both Gatso and Dichout were just along for the ride.

A total of 196 cars set off from Noordwijk with some of the oldest cars being the Ford Club Cabriolet V8 of Ton and Geerd van Helden and the Citroen Traction Avant of Ruud and Miriam Wesselink, both cars dating from 1937. Beating even that though was Bob and Willem Meijer's 1936 Riley Sprite. The entry was overwhelmingly Dutch, with six British crews the next biggest contingent, easily outnumbering the Germans, who only have to come from across the border but seem disinclined to do so.

From Noordwijk the route took the rally to Bergen op Zoom in southern Holland, then to Chaam and La Roche in the Belgian Ardennes. The route was the usual mix of long road sections, special regularity stages and a number of secret routes with time controls. The next day saw sections of three countries covered with more of Belgium, Luxembourg and then a section through northen France to Turckheim in the French Vosges which, with rather unusual Dutch hyperbole, featured a 1000 lakes section.

The fourth day required the crews to cover the 350km stage from Turckheim to Monschau in Germany with the final day taking the remaining cars back to Noordwijk via Brooklands Classic Cars at Veenendaal with Munda and Roriffe well in charge.

Cees Willemse and Anton Vermeulen's 1961 Jaguar XK150 was just one of the 195 cars to follow in the wake of the Belgian winners, Munda and Roriffe

Oldest entry bar one was the Wesselinks' 1937 Citroen Traction Avant, left. One of over 20 big Healeys, right, leaving the Hotel des Vosges in Turckheim

Gatsonides' Zephyr was not the only one in rally; this is Frits Swinkels' Zephyr Six, left, like Gatso's car a 1953 model. Schippers' 1959 Healey 3000 is seen, right

First day of term

*In Britain, the VSCC Silverstone meeting in April is the
traditional curtain-raiser to the historic racing season. This year,
says PETER TOMALIN, it produced a particularly bright start
— and some interesting thoughts on where the sport is heading*

Ah, the glorious uncertainty of April, VSCC and Silverstone. For the historic racing fraternity, those three magical words are as likely to send a shiver down the spine as to bring a glow to the heart. For those who watch, there's the all-too-seasonal prospect of black clouds scudding across dismal skies, of biting winds and plastic teacups clasped in frozen hands. For those who race, there's the equally unappetising likelihood of a track lashed by driving rain. Or worse; two years ago, it snowed.

But this year, the faithful were well rewarded. Oh, it did snow; but that was on Friday, during practice. By mid-morning on Saturday, race day, the clouds had lifted. By mid-afternoon the circuit was bathed in Spring sunshine and early morning Barbours and quilted waistcoats had given way to shirtsleeves. Winter was at an end, and even the Silverstone paddock looked inviting as the cars were wheeled out for another new year.

That is as it should be for this Itala Trophy Meeting – like the first day of a new term. For the drivers, hopes are high; all things are possible. But as with any meeting of the Vintage Sports Car Club, the racing is only part of it. For the follower, it is time to shake off winter blues, renew old friendships and make the annual pilgrimage for that first fix of Castrol R and blaring exhausts. And there, the meeting rarely disappoints. . .

After the appetiser – a five-lap scratch race in which Gregor Fisken edged Dan Margulies' Alta home ahead of Keith Knight's ERA/Riley – it was straight into the serious business of the 1950s Sports Racing Cars: Frank Sytner in Sir Anthony Bamford's D-type, Gary Pearson in a Lister Jaguar, Barrie 'Whizzo' Williams in the Lynx-prepared Tojeiro Jaguar, a host of other Jaguars, various Lotuses, and a cluster of Italian exotics, from Birdcage to Testa Rossa. And along with the old hands, some new faces, most notably the Earl of March, down in the programme as plain Charles March, and driving his first circuit race in the pretty little Lola-Climax.

The vagaries of the weather brought a twist to the grid. David Pennell, who had practised later than most, in the dry, found himself unexpectedly on pole in his D-type, but after a couple of laps, normal service was resumed: Sytner chased by Pearson with Williams a close third, hotly pursued by Robert Brooks in the Lotus 15. It was hard, fast, competitive racing – exactly what the crowd wanted to see. Ten exhilarating laps later, Sytner took the flag, just half a second ahead of Pearson. Pennell himself had enjoyed a rare old scrap, with Valentine Lindsay's D; indeed there had been close racing all through the field.

But there is a yawning gulf between the quickest and the slowest – some of whom had been lapped twice in ten short laps of the Club circuit. And this is something that Frank Sytner, for one, thinks should be addressed by the race organisers. The former Touring Car champion, now a regular front-runner in historic racing, reckons it's a safety issue. 'I'm not criticising the drivers, more the officials,' he says. 'But those with minimal experience should be given very, very strong advice on how to handle being lapped two or three times in a race – how they should stay on their line, use their mirrors. The marshals with the blue flags have a great responsibility too. At the moment, I don't think anyone is taking it seriously enough. And accidents will be caused. . .'

In the usually cosy world of historic racing, this is controversial stuff, but it is an inevitable consequence of historic racing gaining a higher profile. Sytner predicts more top-flight drivers will join the ranks, and sooner or later, he believes, it will be necessary to separate novices in slower cars from the hard chargers.

'In certain races,' he says, 'there is such a difference between the older, slower cars and the newer, faster ones that I think it's

Martin Stretton (Talbot) chases Ivan Dutton (Bugatti) in one of the duels of the day, for the Itala and Lanchester Trophies

time to look at the entries. The cars at the front are often the most valuable, with the biggest back-up and the biggest team. They have owners who want to see them go quickly. The crowd want that too. They want to see a D-type cornering quickly, drifting.'

But is there a growing gulf between the drivers? Some say the likes of Sytner should be more laid back, more tolerant of those just starting out. Up to a point, Frank agrees. 'Yes,' he says, 'we do take it seriously. But not to anything like the extent that some people think. In touring cars, keeping your seat next week might depend on winning. Now that I'm involved purely in the historic side, winning is no longer everything. For me, the great pleasure is still to be lucky enough to drive these fabulous cars.

'Maybe it's not traditionally a part of the racer's mind-set, but at the age of 52, I'm prepared to put my hands up and say, OK, perhaps I've been trying too hard. But I'd still like to carry on driving these cars for a long time. And yes, some of us do experience the red mist, but I think there's a growing realisation that we've all got to give more consideration to other people in the race. There are other people out there having fun, too.'

The beam on Charles March's face suggested that he was definitely one of them. His Silverstone debut brought a perfectly respectable mid-field finish, but from the way his family and friends descended on him in the paddock you could be forgiven for thinking he'd won. His relief was tangible. 'I don't know what to say really. It's good to have got one out of the way!' he laughed. 'It was very wet for practice yesterday, and then it started snowing. I started about halfway down the grid – about twentieth of around forty cars. Then I had a very poor start, and I've no idea where I ended up, but the car went very well.'

Was he nervous before the race? 'A bit. I'll be a lot less nervous next time because I'll know what to expect. I did my first race about two years ago, in Robert Brooks' Lotus 15, and that was actually in the snow! Not a pleasant experience. We got out onto the grid and it literally started snowing, huge flakes sticking to your visor. I came off after about three laps; so that doesn't really count, because I couldn't see anything. At least I know now what it's like to have other cars around. . .'

He's got a good car in the Lola Mk 1, bought in 1995, and

Above: no fewer than four fabulous Maserati 250Fs lined up for the Peter Collins Race. This is Nick Mason's

originally raced by Angus Clydesdale. Having stood virtually idle since the 1970s, it was subject to a major rebuild by Terry Hall and Hall & Fowler, and according to Charles March it is now 'a very sweet handling, easy car. It's fantastic around Goodwood, but we've only had it out once properly there. It's just out of the box, to be honest. Not having really done a race before, and never having driven at Silverstone before, I'm just feeling my way'.

So it's a steep learning curve? 'Very steep. Precipitous, I think, would be the word.' And is he hooked on this racing thing now? 'I'll let you know in a few races' time. . .'

Robert Brooks, auctions man and regular racer, is also bubbling with enthusiasm: 'April Silverstone – it's great, isn't it? Especially when you get a day like today. The year doesn't really get going until now. There's a start-of-term feeling, a special atmosphere. And it's always over-subscribed.

'This year there seem to be lots of new cars and new people; I've seen plenty of yellow novice squares with black crosses on. But new blood means new interest, and that's important. We should be bending over backwards to help them, and I have to say, I found the general standard of driving high. It's all about VSCC members enjoying their sport, and the sport has to grow'.

Brooks' Lotus had had its usual winter health check: 'David persuaded me to have a rollover hoop on it, but apart from that all he did was clean out the engine, take the diff out, because we keep eating diffs, and weld the chassis, because it cracks every year...'

Back on the track, Robin Baker's Delage, with its amusing

27-litre Hispano Suiza V12 aero engine, had harried Mark Walker's GN-based 'Parker' special all the way to the line in the Vintage Allcomers Race, before the second major event of the day – the Peter Collins Race for post-war single seaters. No fewer than four Maserati 250Fs lined up in this one, along with various Connaughts and Coopers, a Dino Ferrari and a P3 Alfa; but it was the glorious V16 BRM that blared away from the flag.

These cars didn't always run well, but when they do they're a wonderful sight and sound. As Amschel Rothschild opened up a useful lead over Philip Walker's Lotus 16, the BRM was clearly on full song, but by lap eight of 12 it was starting to sound a little off-key, and Walker was closing. Rothschild held on to win by a mere 1.7 seconds, and afterwards he was clearly delighted: 'We've had the V16 a great number of years now, and it's finally going well. It feels a very modern car compared with others of the same era.' Tragically, it proved to be one of his last appearances before his untimely death a few weeks later, at his own hand and apparently as a result of deep stress over business worries.

On the racing front, his worries were limited. For the BRM's success, he credited Crossthwaite & Gardner, who were responsible for its preparation and obvious fine fettle. But what of those drivers who circumstances dictate do their own preparation? For them, on more of a shoestring, days like these can be immensely rewarding – or equally frustrating.

Tony Stephens, who campaigns Bill Morris's ex-Bira ERA R12B, spent the end of last season re-jigging the chassis after the

gearbox input shaft broke. 'I discovered the 'box was out of line with the engine – probably a legacy of an old accident. That took a lot of fiddling. Then the car started to be plagued with a misfire. But it's all character-forming.'

Stephens operates from a tow-truck-cum-mobile-work-shop-cum-motorhome, a 15-year-old Chevrolet ambulance bought for £1500. There's no big back-up; the pit crew is wife Alison, and daughter Olivia, six. 'It's hard work,' he admits, 'but you can run an ERA by yourself, providing it's fitted with a starting handle so you don't need pushers. The thing is, you then have to chase after the car because the drag of the gearbox carries it away, but I've got quite good at running after it and jumping in...'

He says he always wanted to be a racing driver, had some of his ambition crushed when he grew up to be 6ft 4in, and eventually fell into historic racing. 'That was about 25 years ago. At the time you could get a good old car for next to nothing.' Although Tony is a successful businessman, he doesn't have a huge budget. 'If I'm lucky, I can get away with spending £5000 a season. But there are people here who can spend £30,000 a year easily.'

Bill Morris first offered him the chance to drive an ERA in 1976, and he took over R12B last year. 'Problem is,' he says, 'when you've got a car that you know is good, then you find out whether you're any good as a driver. I think I was born with a bit too much imagination...'

Alas for Tony, his misfire returned (later diagnosed as a loose valve seat) to put him out of the third big event of the day -

A winning smile from Frank Sytner, left, who was in sparkling form with the D-type Jaguar in the 1950s Sports Car Race

*A stroll
through the
car park at
Silverstone
turns up
all sorts of
delights
- like this
extraordinary
rear-engined
V8 Tatra*

the Patrick Lindsay Pre-War Historic Scratch Race. There had been several excellent support races. The five lap handicap was notable for boasting a Schumacher on pole (Cecil in a Talbot rather than Michael in a Ferrari) and an inspired drive by Paul Smeeth in the rapid Richard Bolster Special who couldn't quite catch Peter Whenman's winning Lagonda. Then there was an excellent duel between Ivan Dutton (Bugatti 35B) and Martin Stretton (Talbot) for the Itala and Lanchester Trophies.

But it was the Patrick Lindsay Race that had the crowds deserting the paddock to take up vantage points at Brooklands and Copse. Another good field was headed by Lindsay's son Ludovic with his late father's famous mount Remus, the ex-Bira ERA. In the event, there were several retirements and Martin Stretton produced an exhibition drive in the ex-Furmanik 1.5-litre Maserati, with Mark Gillies (Brooke Special) and Lindsay in vain pursuit. Stretton rarely had the Maserati in a straight line, his car control something to behold. The man is a star.

Back in the paddock, Ludovic reveals he had been having problems with Remus. 'A spark plug started cracking up at the beginning of the race, so I couldn't pull more than 5200 revs. It was the tenth anniversary of the race, which made it doubly frustrating.' Still, he's as enthusiastic as ever about the coming season, talking of plans to drive the Turtle Drilling Special at Goodwood. The 1960 Indianapolis car has only two gears, but with 450bhp from its 4.2-litre Offenhauser four, it should make an interesting hillclimb car. . . He gives the appearance of a relaxed, Corinthian attitude to racing and he isn't one for lengthy test sessions. 'You can treat this like modern racing and develop the car', he says, 'but to me that's rather anally retentive. Historic cars should be kept that way. Make them safer, but the more you develop them, the more you lose. It's also cheaper not to!

'Of course you want to win, and if you do well you're very proud. But you're still the same person if you don't. There are a few inflated egos, but people like Martin Stretton don't have an ego problem. Most important, if they don't do well, they'll still be back next year. And the standard of driving here is incredibly high, because these cars aren't easy. Personally, I look forward to these events from months ahead. We all do. It's very involving. You're surrounded by lots of friends, there's always something to see, and you're still buzzing two weeks later.'

If he has concerns, they're with increased commercialisation and creeping officialdom. 'Silverstone in some ways has sold out to Formula 1. They put corporate hospitality before the ordinary spectator.' Tony Stephens has similar reservations: 'I think Silverstone is a bit spoiled for historic racing. The gravel traps aren't good news for us. You can only really afford to go in forwards or backwards, otherwise you'll be over.'

Frank Sytner, a director of Silverstone, understands some of these concerns. 'The FIA are becoming more and more involved,' he agrees, 'and the sort of people who own and run these cars don't want to be ruled and governed. But Silverstone is still a circuit run by enthusiasts for enthusiasts. The BRDC is working hard to give the drivers more challenge and the spectators more spectacle. We just have to remind ourselves that these events are fun.'

And there's the crux of it. Every year, historic racing gets bigger. The spectacle of, say, Martin Stretton balancing the Maserati in a power-slide makes it look so natural. The powers that govern this sport have a similar balancing act to perform in the coming months, keeping the real enthusiast – driver and spectator alike – happy, while the profile of historic racing grows. I went home from April VSCC Silverstone happy. From where I'm standing, the sport looks healthier than ever.

British E-Type of David Vine and David Edmund in thoroughly French scenery

Tour de France Auto

There is a Tour de France on four wheels as well as on two, now nearing its hundredth birthday and bringing back echoes of the great Tours of old. RICHARD MEADEN spent four days chasing the action from Paris to Nice, on road, circuit and special stage

For four glorious days in June, the roads of France host one of the most challenging events on the classic calendar - the Tour de France Auto. This year's is officially headlined as the 55th, with the modern retrospective now in its fifth year, but its spirit dates back almost a century, to the pioneering race of 1899. That was followed by a series of similar events from 1906 to 1914, and the Tour was resurrected after World War I with races from 1922 to 1937 becoming a marathon test for ever more sporting cars.

Reborn in 1951, it became even more prestigious, more competitive, and began to attract entries from the likes of Ferrari, Jaguar, Aston Martin and Maserati. From 1952 it adopted the classic format of demanding road sections punctuated by circuit and hillclimb tests which gave it its greatest days through the 1950s, 1960s and into the 1970s - until first the oil crisis then less spectacular races and more mundane entries let it peter out in the mid 1980s, just as it passed its 50th running.

In 1992 the Tour was revived again, in retrospective guise; and from 128 cars in that first of the current

series, it has never looked back. This year, it attracted almost 180 cars, split between the full-race FIA class, and the more sedate regularity class. All follow the same route, with closed circuits and spectacular special stages, but the regularity cars are in theory pitted only against the clock, and the FIA cars race against one another.

On the Tuesday before Wednesday's start, competitors gather in the centre of Paris, in the shadow of the Eiffel Tower. By evening, the Trocadero is surrounded by classic competition cars, and the variety is amazing. Where else, for instance, could you see a competition Ferrari Daytona parked next to a Lancia 037 Rallye, or a 250 GTO sharing the tarmac with a Mini Cooper S? Even overcast skies and heavy rain can't dampen the atmosphere, and the rainbow framing the Tower simply hints at the colour and spectacle the next four days hold in store.

Wednesday morning brings added urgency. 24 hours earlier, drivers and co-drivers had sipped champagne while support crews applied decals and polished hand-beaten alloy panels. Now they work together with a purpose. For the FIA teams especially, more than 1500

road miles, plus circuit races and special stages will be a gruelling test of mechanical strength, physical stamina and smart logistics.

At 9am the Tour kicks-off. One by one, 176 cars are waved away from the Trocadero (FIA cars first), into the Paris rush. The mind boggles at the thought of mixing temperamental racing cars worth as much as a large lottery win into the scrum of Renault 5s, but helped by a crack team of fearless Gendarmes on bright blue BMW motorcycles, the competitors head for the outskirts of the capital and the famous circuit of Montlhéry.

The track's impossibly steep banking is an awesome sight, even when it's empty. Fill it with a flat-out train of great sports racing cars of the '50s, '60s and '70s, and it makes the hairs on the back of your neck prickle; but Siggy Brunn in his Viper Green Porsche 911 2.8 RSR masters the damp and tricky concrete bowl to take the flag, while David Piper's 275LM Ferrari and Gerard Larousse's super-quick 911S are both impressive. But as Larousse is a double Le Mans winner, his pace isn't entirely unexpected.

From Montlhéry, the competitors begin the first of many long road sections on the four-day drive to Nice. From the outskirts of Paris they head south west, towards Le Mans, to reassemble for either a race or a regularity run on the Bugatti Circuit. First to arrive are the FIA cars, mostly piloted by the co-drivers, giving the drivers a breather before the next race.

Le Mans is a highlight for many drivers. Some of these cars actually raced in the 24-hours, so this is a spritual home for them. It's early evening when the FIA race gets under way, and as the warm sun sinks low over the grandstands, the sound of Porsche RSRs, Daytonas and Shelby Mustangs reverberates around the paddock. Few motor racing experiences can be more special.

The first night is spent in the vicinity of Le Mans, and most crews meet up for the evening meal at the circuit museum. The intense schedule and long distances mean most will retire from the gathering early, but it is a Tour tradition that the social side of the four-day event is almost as important as the driving. . .

The cars are kept in the Le Mans paddock overnight. Most support crews and drivers will be up before 5am, in readiness for

David Piper and Bernard Duc's 275LM eventually came home in 30th place in spite of an early, non-damaging visit to the gravel

Variety is the spice of the Tour and the route is superbly scenic. Bellm's drive in the Aston was spectacular, but not quite as spectacular as the Montlhery banking. Left, is the regularity winning 300SL

GT40 of ultimate 'winners' McErlain and Merifield, in Montresor. 356 Carrera of Unterberger and Kozca was a change from 911s. Mustangs in the mountains are fine matched pair of Shelby GT350s

the second day, which involves more lengthy road sections, a closed road hillclimb, and a race at the private circuit of Le Mas du Clos. Despite bleary eyes, the early morning drive to the breakfast halt is worth getting up for. With a chill dawn mist surrendering to the warming rays of a bright June sun, the fast open roads and wonderful French countryside make this the most memorable road section of the Tour so far.

Memorable for others, too. Old race cars need a lot of fuel, and many filling station proprietors find their forecourts clogged with exotic, high octane machinery. These impromptu pit stops also allow local villagers a glimpse of the Tour, and as the morning ticks by, excited school children relish the chance to wave at the racing cars and miss a few lessons.

The original Tour de France was as much a gastronomic crawl as a motor race. In keeping with such a civilised practice, today's breakfast stop is held in the manicured grounds of the spectacular Chateau de Valencay. It's a relaxed start to an otherwise hectic day, and the crews make the most of the respite.

From the Chateau it's no more than an hour or so's fast road

driving to the first timed section of the day, at Sainte-Sévère. The assembly area is nothing more than a dusty car park, which allows spectators to get close to cars and crews. Those teams that take the Tour seriously have little time to talk. The stage is only 6km long but it's fast, confined, and there are sharp corners waiting to punish the unwary. The co-driver's road book has them marked, but it's better to be safe than sorry, so most crews can be seen buried in the books until it's their turn to drive the stage.

The FIA cars, as usual, simply have to attack the quickest time. Regularity crews have to predict their time before the start and then do their best to match the prediction. The best manage it to the second. The pressure on these crews is immense.

Now it's approaching the half way point, and although a few cars (most notably the second Ferrari 250LM, driven by Gary Pearson and owned by celebrated Ferrari collector Brandon Wang) have dropped by the wayside, the vast majority of the field reaches the amazing Mas du Clos circuit in good fettle.

Cut into rolling countryside west of Vichy, it is a perfectly manicured, pocket-sized, Nurburgring-style track. Again, the green 911 RSR of Siggy Brunn wins the FIA section, although Larousse is performing well in his 911, and the wonderful winged competition Daytonas of Racing Team Holland put on a thunderous display. David Piper is still pressing on in his 275LM, and has a slight coming together with Martyn Konig, who is moving up the field in another glorious 2.8 911 RSR.

Vichy provides the second overnight stop. It has been a long day, and the morning will come a few hours too soon for many FIA crews. As usual, they are the first to set off, this time heading for the twisting, hilly Charade circuit, a tangle of tarmac amongst the volcanic outcrops of the Pau de Gravenoire - source of Volvic mineral water. It's a stupendous track, but almost devoid of run-off. Unyielding Armco and concrete walls line it, but even this fails to inhibit some of the more flamboyant drivers. Ray Bellm, a racer more ususally found in the driving seat of a

McLaren F1, rarely has his Aston Martin DB4 GT pointing in the direction of travel, wrestling this brawny old sports car around in spectacular, tail-sliding style. A true showman. . .

After the tight confines of Charade, the Tour continues south towards Avignon. The next timed stage is a tough five-hour drive away; and just when they need their wits about them, many crews are beginning to feel the pace. The Burzet stage is the most daunting of the Tour thus far. A narrow 16km stretch of road running across the mountains, it is extremely challenging, and certainly not for the faint hearted. So severe is the terrain, and so steep the drops, that many crew members suffer badly with vertigo. If ever the phrase 'don't look down' applied, it's here.

Burzet claims the leading 911 RSR of Siggi Brunn, when co-driver John Lewis misses his braking point, and slides backwards off the road. Considering the terrain, they were lucky to escape with no more than a cracked sump and engine casings. Many others were lucky to avoid a similar fate.

The final overnight halt is in the walled city of Avignon. The weather has deteriorated and by morning it's raining hard - a great shame as the Tour is about to take in one of the greatest hill-climbs in the world. Mont Ventoux is a mighty special stage, climbing for 9km into the mountains; but damp roads and patchy fog deter many from making a real charge. Some of the leading FIA cars, nonetheless, are spectacularly quick, pressing on in a desperate bid to gain places on the last day.

But if Mont Ventoux was tough, Castellane was bordering on the impossible. A huge 16km stage, the road clings to the side of the mountains, with huge drops, sparse barriers and some corners so tight that you'd think twice about running around them on foot. With hindsight the stage shouldn't have been run, and shortly after the FIA cars entered the stage, disaster struck.

First Martyn Konig crashed his RSR into the Armco and out of a sure third place. Then a lightweight E-type and a 250 SWB came to grief in similar circumstances. Sadly worse was to come. Paul Grist and Burkhard von Schenk were caught out by the same corner that claimed Konig, but instead of coming to an abrupt halt in the armco, they vaulted it and crashed into the

Winner on time Larousse takes a break, victor by book McErlain storms Mont Ventoux. GTO leads 911, lightweight E and Aston through typical mountain section

ravine, comprehensively destroying their Maserati A6GCS. Both were thrown clear, but Grist suffered a broken shoulder blade. When the wreck of the Maserati was recovered it became clear things could have been a lot worse. The stage was declared void, and the remainder of the field sent to the last stage, at La Turbie.

Set on the coast within sight of Nice, La Turbie is a short sprint up the meandering sea-view climb. It's by no means easy though, as a fresh sprinkling of rain makes the road surface slick and greasy. And it's typical of the Tour to throw up such a test of concentration within sight of the finish.

As tired cars and crews reach Nice in dribs and drabs, Larousse heads the field from Pieter Boel and Guus Bierman's Dutch Daytona, but as the rules say only a pre-1966 car can be overall winner, the third placed duo of Andrew Merifield and David-Patrick McErlain in a Ford GT40 takes FIA honours, while unnerringly precise German drivers Richard Weiland and George Walter are regularity winners in their Mercedes 300SL.

It had its share of incidents, but the 1996 Tour de France was as exciting, demanding and intense as it has always been. You get the impression that no-one would want it any other way.

28 April-2 May
Mini Monte

Thirty years, forty years or fifty years, it doesn't much matter: all you need these days, it seems, is an anniversary - always the perfect hook on which to hang another, welcome classic event. And that's how Philip Young looked back thirty years to when the Minis won one of their incredible Monte Carlo triumphs and decided to celebrate it with a Minis-only re-run.

An inspired idea, it struck a cord with hundreds of Mini owners. For some it was only a dream, but others decided that they would go on the trip of a lifetime come what may. That was certainly Tim Grayer's view. A while ago he'd acquired a £60 wreck of a Mini requiring a total rebuild but optimistically entered for the event anyway; and, as it does, time had almost run out. By the time the car was finished, only four days were left before the start of the rally for the 22-year-old to get acclimatised. But it turned out to be more than enough. Embarking on his first ever drive abroad, let alone his first rally, Grayer, with equally inexperienced co-driver Adrian Elkin, set out to have a good time, found themselves leading after three days and kept it all together to reach Monte Carlo as the winners.

So it must have been an easy run for complete novices to win, mustn't it? Well yes, but only up to a point. In reality, nothing can make the mountain routes that the Monte Minis took really easy. The Col du Turini doesn't suddenly get straightened out just because it's only hosting a retro run, and you don't set fire

Fantastic scenery but not much time to look at it. 1995 Cooper of Neil and Amanda Long just made it into the top twenty, having lost test penalty points between Reims and Aix

Hugh and Janet Wylie's 1969 Cooper S was one of the wolves in sheep's clothing, in this case with a 1380 engine; but size isn't everything and the Wylies finished 32nd

Strong British contingent with everything ahead of them on Dover docks. Age wasn't a problem, and nor was competition history - most cars were near standard

to your brakes, as Grayer did, unless you're trying hard. Nor was the weather always kind. As the Minis got to that famous stage, they were greeted by lightning and heavy rain; but their ability in atrocious conditions is what made the Minis great in the first place, so it seemed perfectly appropriate.

At least the likes of Grayer had a gentle start as the cars left Calais, where the competitors from France, Germany, Holland, Norway and Luxembourg joined them for the 1440km route with an easy run through the flat countryside of northern France, past the faded glory of the Reims GP circuit. But by Aix les Bains it had already become apparent that things were getting tougher - two ex BMC mechanics hadn't, after all, been brought along just for the ride, and they were soon using their knowledge of every Mini nut and bolt to keep up with numerous running repairs.

Paul Easter, a Monte winner for real in a Mini some decades ago, put his knowledge as one of the best navigators in the business to good use in constructing this event's route from a number of elements used on Montes past - culminating with the cars descending into Monte Carlo down the wonderfully fast twists and turns of the famous La Turbie hillclimb.

Keeping Easter company in the nostalgia game was Mini GRX 5D, a genuine works 1275cc Cooper S. More than seventy Minis were once works cars, but this is the actual one disqualified from the 1966 Monte for, of all nit-picking details, having the wrong headlight arrangement according to the French organisers. Back in the 1960s it was driven to several victories by Paddy Hopkirk, but it now belongs to Simon Howes and lives with him in the hills outside Monte Carlo. Howes, like Grayer, was on his first competitive event, but GRX 5D, with more experience, made it all the way once again.

One agreeably relaxed feature about the Mini Monte was a totally flexible attitude which didn't restrict the entry to Minis of a certain age but welcomed one and all. That meant the likes of Grayer's late 1970s 1275 was battling it out with both older models and newer cars - such as Luxembourg driver Juliette Tenconi's wildly modified 1980s Mini Mayfair, with straight-cut gearbox and 1380cc engine. Ms Tenconi's skills, however, matched the extra power and she took the Coupe des Dames.

Grayer, meanwhile, was not unduly disadvantaged by giving away a considerable amount of horsepower to many rivals. The Mini Monte was not a flat-out race and the trick in these events is making sure you don't drop silly points, for example on the steep descent from Mount Granier, a regularity section on which cars had to average only 32kph. If you can display the iron will and restraint to do that, you deserve to win. And so did the event. It looks set to run and run, whatever the anniversary...

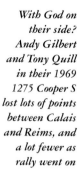

With God on their side? Andy Gilbert and Tony Quill in their 1969 1275 Cooper S lost lots of points between Calais and Reims, and a lot fewer as rally went on

Juliette Tenconi and husband Jim on the long Reims straight, with the scream of straight-cut gears, left. Phil Welland, right, and Andrew Shepherd came home in fifth

Don't be fooled by names, on right is actually Stephen Smith and Michael Corbett, who finished 42nd. Left, en route to 48th are Hubert and Nathalie Grouset

Haynes RACMSA Two-Day Classic 27-28 April

Just down the road from Haynes Publishing's headquarters in Sparkford, near Yeovil, Somerset, is the expanding Haynes Motor Museum, which now houses more than 300 cars and motorcycles, covering everything from Isetta bubblecar to Graham Hill's Lola Cosworth F1 car. It is an impressive collection, and testimony to John Haynes' enthusiasm for old cars. His is a genuine enthusiasm for using what he collects, too. His cars don't just sit gathering dust in the museum; many are regularly driven and, not least, many of them regularly appear on the ever increasing number of classic car runs that now spice up the calendar.

Now Haynes themselves have added to that number, by sponsoring the RAC Motor Sport Association's Two-Day Classic run in late April, for cars of more than twenty years old, and this year covering a route of some 350 miles in the Welsh borders and the south west corner of England.

With Haynes being based in Somerset, it made sense for the event to centre on the West Country. The organisers stressed that the run is not a race, but just intended to be, as they put it, 'an interesting drive between pleasant stopping places'. In fact this year it was two interesting drives, as the huge entry of over 330 cars was often divided into two groups to avoid congestion, even though all the cars stopped at the same places.

The bulk of those present were the always to be expected MGs, TRs, Austin Healeys and E-types - with the odd unusual interloper such as the Ian Tisdale Chevrolet Corvair, Quentin Gray's Allard K1, James Smith's K2, and Karl and Annette Ludvigsen's 1937 4.8-litre Cord 812.

Oldest car in the field was Hugh and Judy Smith's 1925 3-litre Speed Model Bentley, the most recent within the twenty year rule was Jonathan Gordon's 1976 Triumph Stag, but there were a few youngsters beyond that, up to a 1995 Porsche, so the rules were obviously fairly relaxed. There were also the odd Clyno and Jowett, Lea Francis and Swallow Doretti, even a sprinkling of Ferraris - and John Haynes himself was there with his 1959 Jaguar XK150.

All started in a single convoy, at the fairly civilised hour of nine in the morning, from Town Park in Telford town centre, soon reaching the Loton Park Hillclimb just west of Shrewsbury, and then on to Powys Castle, Welshpool, which was just about the route's furthest point west. It was there that the massive entry divided onto its separate routes, labelled red and green, the reds thereafter going via Kerry, Clun and Ludlow, the greens via Newtown, Knighton and Presteigne, before linking up again at Berrington Hall and joining forces at the Prescott Hillclimb, a few miles north of Cheltenham.

There, although the vast majority of drivers wouldn't previously have experienced Prescott, and the event was, of course, non-competitive, they were about to discover a hillclimb which to the unitiated looks easy - until you try it, when you quickly realise why even experienced hillclimbers make mistakes. It's all part of the character of the event, of course.

From the Cheltenham overnight stop and the social rigours of the Pitville Pump Room, the cars then headed south again to the Castle Combe circuit near Chippenham and a different kind of challenge from Prescott, while after calling at Wilton House near Salisbury for one of the events more cultural checkpoints, it was on to another hillclimb, at Gurston Down near Broadchalk before heading, via Shaftesbury and Wincanton back to the Haynes Motor Museum and a very relaxed finish.

And of course, although there were no winners and no losers, there were plenty of exciting tales to be told, and plenty of people already laying plans for next year's return. . .

The Dovey family's immaculate 1955 3-litre Aston Martin DB2/4 near the top of Prescott hillclimb on Saturday afternoon: the hill isn't as easy to learn as it looks

One of the oldest cars on the event, John Peckham and George Till's lovely 1935 Alvis Firebird

Style statement: Paul Eccles' handsome 1963 Studebaker Avanti R2 was one of several nice Americans

Haute Carrosserie

by

Our artisans are acknowledged
masters of the skilful art of
coachbuilding, offering
unsurpassed experience from
the production and restoration
of coachwork for the worlds
most important historic
automobiles, to the research
design and build of modern
coachwork. From the
Edwardian Silver Ghost
for the discerning
enthususiast, to the
modern touring
limousine for the
Nobility and
Heads of
State.

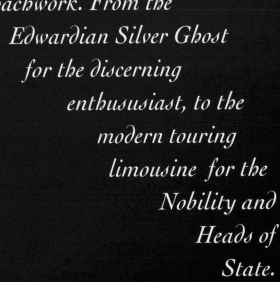

HOOPER-CRAILVILLE INTERNATIONAL
Coachbuilders

Canal Yard, Hayes Road, Southall, Middlesex UB2 5NA U.K. Tel: (+44) 181 574 7727 Fax: (+44) 181 571 9460

4-6 MAY
Tour de Corse

A pleasant jaunt through spectacular countryside, with plenty of time to indulge in automotive nostalgia? Forget it. The Tour de Corse Retro 40 was organised by John Brown, who is well known for his classic events but clearly bears a good-natured grudge against anyone driving an old car.

He is the same man, for instance, who each year persuades apparently perfectly sane people to drive from Lands End to John O'Groats in mid-winter in the infamous LE JOG, while sending them on complicated detours through dark Welsh forests at night and depriving them of sleep for days.

And this year he did the seemingly impossible. He designed an even more demanding event than that, along with a tougher than ever schedule and an equally punishing route through the mountains of Corsica, to celebrate the fortieth anniversary of the first Tour de Corse.

Pure sadism? Well the competitors probably thought so at the time but the satisfaction gained in actually making it to the finish of an event as tough as this one turned out to be will live on for years, where the memory of an easy drive soon fades.

To enjoy that glow of satisfaction, of course, you first have to get to the finish, and only just over half the cars entered actually made it over the three days to the end of the 1600km route - an attrition rate which led some to suggest that this year's Retro route was actually harder than the 'modern' Tour de Corse rally which took place the weekend before. . .

Certainly the Retro covered the whole island - from Ajaccio in the south to Macinaggio at the very end of the northern peninsula. And in his usual style, John Brown threw in a difficult night navigation section, in this case over 300km in the Castagniccia region. Naturally, too, he scheduled that right at the end of the rally, over the Sunday night and Monday morning. By then the drivers and navigators would be at their most tired (and their most hungry - with meal stops being conspicuously absent), having started at 7am Sunday morning with the prospect of finishing from seven onwards the next morning, as the culmination of 24 hours concentrated driving and navigating.

Why Corsica? Well in Brown's view the Alps are now far too busy a location in which to try and recreate the old style

Mini Cooper of Richard Martin-Hurst and Wim van Koningsveld is well suited to tight roads but was beaten into second by power and agility of hard-driven and impeccably navigated Tiger

Alpine rallies, while Corsica still has most of what the Alps can offer, except the crowds. Its empty and very demanding roads have plenty of mountain sections, snow capped peaks, high cliffs with sea views, and an endless supply of hairpin bends to maintain the Alpine illusion for crews and spectators alike, while the local population invariably provide an enthusiastic welcome.

This year, that recipe was enough to attract 36 crews. Some were hardened competitors like Ron Gammons, while at the other extreme there was a ladies Rolls-Royce team aiming to squeeze the not inconsiderable bulk of their Corniche through tight corners barely wider than the car itself. Corsica and Corniche were not the perfect combination but it wasn't the car's bulk that let it down; the Rolls ran a bearing.

While the biggest engine in the rally packed up, however, one of the smallest performed faultlessly as usual. The Jorg Schmidt and Sonya Hetherington Renault Dauphine, a successful veteran of the cold and wet of LE JOG, was perfectly prepared yet again. Its tiny pushrod engine is only mildly modified, its suspension

likewise, but it still finished fifth. The top three were the sort of cars you'd expect to last the distance. Ron Gammons' tough MGB was being navigated by Paul Easter to such good effect that they came third, earning Easter the Tour de Corse Trophy (a curious prize for being 'best competitor who competed on the Tour de Corse between 1956 and 1975'). The dents showed that the MGB hadn't managed to avoid quite all the rocks, and even the competitive Gammons observed that perhaps Mr organiser Brown had made things tougher than they could have been.

Ahead of Gammons came the nimble Mini Cooper of Richard Martin-Hurst and Wim van Koningsveld, which most would have reckoned the ideal car for the route; but, forsaking agility for sheer power, top of the pile was in the slightly unlikely shape of a 1965 Sunbeam Tiger. It was, however, a supreme effort by Jayne Wignall who played down her three-day wrestle with the Tiger and gave all the credit to Kevin Savage's virtually perfect navigation. And if the first running is anything to go by, the Tour de Corse Retro itself looks a real winner, too.

With the real Alps becoming more crowded and less suitable for competitive historic rally events, John Brown found a fine look-alike alternative in the mountains of Corsica. Bart and wife Jolyn Rietbergen's 1962 TR4 was 18th of twenty finishers in one of the toughest events of 1996

Paddy Jones and Tony Longstaff took eighth place in their 1962 Riley 1.5 and second in class - albeit some way adrift of Dauphine

Aston Martin Le Mans of Gerry Leumann and Urs Wursch rolled into a ditch during the night section - with only fairly minor damage

For once, a Porsche wasn't the way to go, although Mike Cornwell and Colin Francis's 1964 356 did finish fourth

A Dauphine won first Tour in 1956. Smith/ Hetherington example, with period works spec, took a class win in 1996

RALLY OF THE LAKES 4-5 May

As the Carling Historic Rally of the Lakes rolled around in early May, the Irish championship had Geoff Crabtree and John Keatley looking strong title contenders - with John Coyne, and Dessie Nutt, reliability permitting, still outside challengers.

Keatley's hopes, too, must have been given a lift when business commitments kept his main Porsche rival away this time, but the Coyne car was there at number two, with Nutt close behind - and the winner expected to come from these three.

Killarney on May Bank Holiday has become a mecca for rally fans, the weather is usually kind, and the Ring of Kerry (for many years southern home for the Circuit) can offer such peerless stages as Moll's Gap, Ballaghbeema, Cora Lake and Dunloe. And if you haven't experienced the Moll's Gap stage first thing on a Sunday morning, you haven't lived. The echo of competition cars thundering up the climb past Ladies View, through the Gap itself and over the crest to Kenmare is an experience that photograph, video or audio tape does scant justice to. Book now for 1997. . .

On this great route, the three 911s soon began their customary charge. For a long time, Coyne and Keatley were only seconds apart, but the luckless Nutt drove his heart out only to have his 911 die under him with fuel pump problems.

The best of the rest, meanwhile, was an unassuming engineer from Carrickfergus, Alan Courtney, whose blue Cortina GT has been christened the 'Lotus Eater', because it often does. And out of retirement and making the trip from Warwick, Les Allfrey and Peter Riching's outing in a Cooper S was of the 'suck-it-and-see' variety but other Irish forays look likely for them, while the Wokingham crew of Barry and Kate Porter also crossed the water, but heavy contact with the Kerry countryside saw a rather secondhand MGB making the trip back.

Into the final stages only eight seconds separated the two leading Porsches, then on the Rockfield stage Coyne snatched second gear and the lever with it. The 12 minutes he lost regaining forward movement assured Keatley of the win, as Coyne slipped back to fifth, wondering how he might repeat his Galway victory.

Second place (and the thrill of trailing the Porsche onto the ramp in Killarney) went to Courtney, and an incident that befell third place man Mervyn Johnson's Cooper S sums up the spirit of the event. On Ballaghbeema he spluttered to a halt out of fuel and out of radio contact with any support crew. John Keatley, risking his own victory, siphoned enough fuel from his thirsty 911 to get the Cooper moving again. That's real sportsmanship.

For the moment it is less a question of whether a 911 will win as which 911 will win. Here it was Keatley and Beckett, as Coyne lost his 911's gearlever

Cooper S driver Mervyn Johnson had winner John Keatley to thank for helping him snatch third place in spite of running out of fuel

Cortinas can still mix it with the Porsches, Coopers and Bs. This is Gerry Freeman and Dermot Quigley looking the part in their GT

Alan Courtney's performance, to take second overall in his near standard looking Cortina, was almost as spectacular as the great stages

The Classic Rally Association

The Classic Rally Association organises some of the most evocative and successful events on the European Calendar, and having now organised some 25 international rallies has acquired a considerable background of organisational experience.

The driving force is Philip Young, who founded the European scene for historic rallying ten year ago with the first of the series of Pirelli Classic Marathons - the first was flagged away from London's Tower Bridge and ran across the Alps and the Dolomites to Cortina d'Armpezzo and returned via Holland for a prize-giving at the RAC Club in London's Pall Mall. It was to stand as one of the longest of the Classic Marathons.

Subsequent editions took in different but evocative mountain climbs from the classic Coupe des Alpes of the 1950s and early Sixties... and attracted some of the great names, such as Moss, Makinen, Hopkirk and from the States, former Indianapolis winner Bobby Unser who all tried to get their hands on an elusive Alpine Cup for a clean sheet. Classic car enthusiasts rubbed shoulders in friendly competition with some of the great names, over such hallowed ground as the Stelvio, Italy's highest pass with its staircase of 48 hairpins, the lonely and rugged Gavia, Croce Domini, first used on the 1958 Alpine Rally, along with circuits such as Hockenheim, Nurburgring and Monza. It was a heady mixture, and Pirelli's public relations support ensured television coverage was extended to more than 40 different countries.

The legacy has been a continually growing historic-rally scene. There are now Pirelli Classic Marathons in Japan, South Africa and New Zealand, and the concept has been copied by other rally organisers.

Today, ten years on from the successful launch of an entirely new form of motor-sport onto an unsuspecting world, Philip Young works out of converted stables, offices a few miles south of Abingdon in the Oxfordshire countryside, along with Peter Browning, former Abingdon Competitions Manager of BMC/Leyland, who has a lifetime of motor-sport management behind him, ranging from club events as director of the B.R.S.C.C. at Brands Hatch, to Formula One. He has managed rally teams from as far as Kenya's Safari to the epic long distance marathons such as the original '68 London to Sydney and the remarkable 1970 London to Mexico.

It's a busy office. There are more than 3,000 names on the books of the Classic Rally Association, and events range from the mildly competitive but very strong on the "fun" side of driving a classic car such as the Mini Monte, the Classic Cup which has raised more than ú30,000 for the Wessex Cancer Trust, the Marathon, which has recently spun a road-rally format around the

"A fantastic experience" was how Stirling Moss described it, his MGB pipped by Paddy Hopkirk who rediscovered winning form on the Classic Marathon

mountains of northern Spain as fresh territory, to what is now the biggest event of its kind, the Monte Carlo Challenge.

The Monte attracted 162 starters from more than 170 applicants last winter. It's a remarkable organisational accomplishment as there are as many as six different start venues. As well as the U.K. there is Noorwijke on the Dutch coast, which now attracts half the rally, Oslo sent 20 Norwegians who tend to dominate proceedings once the snow really starts, St. Moritz sees a strong contingent from Switzerland, Germany and Italy... and the format lends itself to new venues for the really adventurous - the 1997 Monte sees the first start from Istanbul.

It's a rally that prides itself in the care of real history - routes penned by Keith Baud have won universal praise. They include much that was familiar to regulars who took part in the "golden era" of the early Sixties. The timing is similar to a late Fifties Monte of the Sunbeam Rapier/Mercedes/TR3 era, for the Rallye Monte Carlo did not adopt scratch timing and total dependancy on special stages until well after Hopkirk delivered the first Mini Cooper victory of 1964.

Keith Baud, and Jeremy Dickson, who has worked full time alongside Philip Young developing historic rallying, provide essential backbone support to the Monte Carlo Challenge's intricate organisation.

Meeting the expectations and demands of responsible organisation demanded by the A.C. de Monaco, who founded the Monte

today's rally have grown with an additional 20 pages!"

"We wanted a totally different concept. The old Montes were perhaps at their best as a road rally, when organisers tried to ensure just about any car could win, not just the works teams with the biggest cheque-book. Nobody else in the historic scene was bothering with cars of the 1950s and early Sixties. It is cheaper by far to build a competitive Mercedes Fintail or a Sunbeam Rapier than a Porsche 911, and we wanted to tackle this with a different approach, but, it had to attract enough competitors.... well, the first two events didn't quite manage to do that, but, we stuck to our guns.

"John Brown, Rob Arthur, Rick Smith, Andrew Bodman, Bob Rutherford have all provided new ideas and support over the years, and now we can look back and appreciate that we got it about right.

Obviously we were able to apply from the beginning some of the lessons learned from the Classic Marathons. It's a happy mixture and works very well." The atmosphere is remarkable.

Drivers in flying jackets, silk scarves, duffle coats, cars right down to the design of the door numbers, all resemble the late 1950s. There is now a pre-1950 Category, with a route similar to a Monte of the Thirties, and a class for cars of a type in production before 1968, which has brought our Mini Cooper S and mix-Sixties cars.

For the coming year, the Classic Rally Association takes on fresh ground and a whole new challenge. The 90th Anniversary of the Peking to Paris.

The route survey is now complete, for a breathtaking adventure drive the full length of China and across the roof of the World of Tibet, with passes as high as 17,000ft and a stop at the foot of the trail to the base camp of Mount Everest, Nepal, 13 river crossings, Himalayan Rally roads, the North West Frontier Passage district of Pakistan, and on across Persia into Turkey and Greece, provide the challenge for 90 cars.

Classic Rallying has certainly come a long way since former Daily Mail and motor-magazine journalist Philip Young decided to revive "real rallying" for historic cars.

Carlo Rallye in 1911, from a British base is a tall order, and vital support within France for permissions from the likes of prefectures and police - the rally runs through several hundred different communities - comes from Monaco's Conference International, who also cater for the hotel bookings of several hundred competitors, as well as producing one of the best prize-givings on the historic calendar when up to 400 thaw out in the warmth and luxury of the Hotel de Paris in Monaco's Casino Square.

The battle through the Alps over some of the most demanding roads Keith Baud and Jeremy Dickson can find, often in the grip of appalling blizzards, sees some epic competition... even when it snows every day, the top ten is split by a mere few seconds.

Since the event first took off, with 65 cars leaving Glasgow under the direction of Clerk of the Course Fred Gallagher who encouraged Young to tackle a Monte for historics, no car has yet reached Monaco with a "clean sheet". The weather helps, of course, but so does a clever balancing act of cut-off dates, for the Monte Carlo Challenge is perhaps unique in declaring outright favouritism for those with an older car.

"When we laid down the format, Fred Gallagher and I thought it would be best if we tried to provide something not already on offer," recalls Philip Young. "We were on a recce for a Classic Marathon on a road to Hockenheim.

Further plans went onto the back of a menu that night ... indeed, we managed to get the entire regulations written on a menu, the final published version is two sides of A4... happy days,

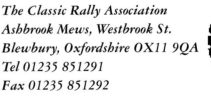

Monte Carlo challenge action always produces an exhilarating event

The Classic Rally Association
Ashbrook Mews, Westbrook St.
Blewbury, Oxfordshire OX11 9QA
Tel 01235 851291
Fax 01235 851292

Mille Miglia

In Italy, there is a very flexible attitude towards reasons for celebration. Plenty of them revolve around good living, many revolve around cars. Combine the two and, as PETER COLLINS discovered, you have the modern Mille Miglia

I think the moment when we finally realised that the 1996 Mille Miglia really was going to be something special was the moment when a grinning Brescian policeman, without so much as a raised eyebrow, moved a no-parking sign out of our way, to allow us to park.

Like thousands of enthusiasts, I've probably read just about everything that has been written about the famous race, but until you're there, little can prepare you for the magic that unfolds over three days during which reality seems to be put on hold. In the UK, simply to ask the authorities for permission to run an event such as this would probably result in arrest; in Italy it is perfect excuse for a celebration, so it was reasonable to expect that pursuing the 1996 re-run could be relied upon to provide plenty of experiences and memories - and we were not disappointed.

For one thing, the Mille Miglia entry is usually superb, in both size and quality. This year, within a total of 338 cars entered, 52 separate marques were represented. Not surprisingly, indigenous makes such as Ferrari and Alfa Romeo were most numerous - with more than forty examples apiece - but Mercedes-Benz (who were one of the main supporters of the event) mustered 42 cars too, ranging from a 1929 7-litre SSK through 300SL prototypes to a 180D saloon of 1954. The Stuttgart firm also persuaded star drivers including Stirling Moss and Jochen Mass to join the team. Porsches were thick on the ground, of course - including a 550A driven by Scheufele from Switzerland, boss of one of the main event sponsors, Chopard, and with former Ferrari GP driver and multiple Le Mans winner Jacky Ickx as his co-driver.

BMW were strongly represented too, the ranks including several cars from their own museum. The Auto Avio 815 replica crewed by Righini and Stancari recreated the first car constructed by Enzo Ferrari's new company in 1940. The Yamaguchis brought their Allard J2X all the way from Japan, while other drivers came from 25 different countries around the world - ranging geographically from New Zealand to Sweden.

Then there were some even rarer marques in the fray, from

1926 Amilcar CGSS driven by the appropriately named Jolly family from Switzerland blurs through the countryside on its way to 220th place

On Monte Subasio, the Sasamotos' 500 TR leads Ardesi and Franchina's pretty little Cisitalia 202 SC coupe

Cisitalia and Cunningham to Nardi and Pegaso, Scarab and Squire; but as is now traditional, two OMs headed the list of entries for the Thursday evening start in Brescia.

From there, the objective, as always, was to cover a route of approximately 1000 miles, linking Brescia with Ravenna, San Marino, Assisi, Rome, Sienna, Florence and ultimately back to Brescia. And in case you are wondering why it is 1000 miles, rather than 1000 kilometres? Well, the original organisers obviously thought that Mille Miglia sounded better then Mille Seicento Chilometri or whatever; and besides, the Romans always did use miles for measuring distances. . .

For 1996, the route ran first via Verona to a night halt at Ferrara. The following day, Friday 10 May, required a 7am start for the first cars, the oldest of them running first on the road. Twelve hours driving time was allowed - to reach Rome by nine in the evening, with a notional two-hour lunch break. Saturday's start was even earlier, at 6.30am, and just over twelve hours driving time was allowed for the return to Brescia. Yet if it is easy to

consider all this as a good 'jolly', it is necessary to reflect that, in the course of 48 hours, more than 300 cars of between forty and seventy years of age is each required to be driven, hard, for one thousand miles. The event has been described as a 'travelling museum', but in reality that undersells everyone involved.

Even the weather plays its part. Study pictures of past events (and listen to the stories of previous participants) and it is clear that rain is always a distinct possibility at some time during the long grind, so it was with plenty of clothing that we set out for Brescia. Snow on the Simplon Pass merely confirmed the possibilities and the morning of scrutineering dawned wet and grey. But all thoughts of workaday problems like rain were dispelled even before we reached Brescia's Piazza Vittoria, by the sight of just one Ferrari 225S burbling purposefully through the traffic.

As we neared the Piazza (where, by tradition, all Mille Miglia scrutineering has taken place since the beginnings of the event), more and more magnificent cars joined the queue, appearing out of side streets like corks out of bottles, until finally the

Things change slowly in Italy, if they change at all. The scene on the way to the Futa Pass could easily pass for the mid 50s

The sun shone in Gubbio and the locals came out to see sights like this TR2 rubbing shoulders with Alfa 8C 2300 and Alfa Monza

jam ground to a halt. Clearly no-one had considered it necessary to close the roads to normal traffic, so competing cars were to be seen using any and every way of maintaining forward progress to avoid the hazzards of overheating or boiling. And this was when that kind policeman moved the no-parking sign for us. . .

Beyond the cars, the first things you notice on approaching the Piazza Vittoria are the cross-braced wooden barriers, so evocative of all those shots of Mille Miglia cars of the past passing through Italian cities, the cheering crowds craning over them to get a better look at their heroes as they howl past at speeds in excess of 100mph on wet city-centre cobbles. For a moment you stop and think of just how they survived, but the fact is that most of the accidents that finally brought the original series of races to an end happened not in towns but out on the open road.

And one other strange thing: for the modern event, there appears to be little or no local publicity; the town of Brescia and its inhabitants were simply carrying on their everyday lives while several hundred priceless vintage and classic sportscars were

Toothy grin and advanced aerodynamics were hallmarks of Cisitalia 202. With big rear fins and side portholes too, it could have been a 50s American classic but is in fact a Mille Miglia veteran. Alfa badge has cross of Milan and shield of Visconti family

C-Type Jaguar of Galeazzi and Ottelli pursued by a Brescia Bugatti - one of the oldest cars in the event and even older than the race itself

Astons, Alfa and Bentley in close formation. Alfas dominated the event before the war; BMW and Mercedes were the only two non-Italian winners of the real race

paraded in their midst. While scrutineering took over the centre of town, bus services were still running and the sight of a Brescian bus driver patiently waiting for a Maserati 300S to be manoeuvred out of his way has to be seen to be believed.

In a way, this too is typical. Through much of its life, the Mille Miglia had the flavour of a merely national, almost local event; extensive international participation was by no means a regular feature. Yet that image of the Mille Miglia as an almost mystical contest held a long way from home only added to the reputation it eventually achieved.

Notable sights here, amongst many, were the incredible 1947 Savonuzzi Cisitalia 202s, with their roof-mounted aerofoils and high, aerodynamic rear wing tips. In all directions there was visual automotive overload. Amongst the chaos that can only mean Italy, a straight-eight Bugatti backfired loudly while being started up, startling a policeman who was valiantly attempting to maintain point-duty just in front of it; and soon after, a C-type Jaguar swept into an adjoining street for all the world as if it was actually competing on one of the original events.

In fact it would be quite easy to spend the whole day in central Brescia, allowing the tide of competing cars to wash over you, while the Mille Miglia proper has yet to begin. . .

Of the three daily starts, only the first takes places in darkness, as it did for the original event. But, unlike the race's glory years, 1996 saw mercifully little in the way of serious incident. One notable accident befell David Cottingham with his Ferrari 212, due to driveshaft failure, but the crew were able to walk away from it. And minor incidents occur frequently, but that is hardly surprising with more than 300 sports racing cars roaming Italy. At the summit of the climb at San Marino, for instance, there is an extremely tight left turn to take the cars to a control

The Mille Miglia stops for breath, left, but everyday life doesn't stop for the Mille Miglia. Crowds can be guaranteed everywhere - cheering Alfa and Lagonda through narrow heart of Urbino, opposite, or seeing Aston Le Mans cresting Raticosa Pass. Former Grand Prix star and Le Mans winner Jochen Mass shared a 300SL

situated at the summit; a potentially very expensive coming together was narrowly avoided when the Ferrari 500 Mondial of Avanzini and Gardelli started to reverse into a three-point turn, unaware that the Porsche 550RS of Schmidt and Distler was immediately behind. The margin of error between smiles and disaster was about the thickness of a fingernail.

On the good news side, former Ferrari Grand Prix driver Clay Regazzoni, piloting a Lancia Aurelia B20, was thoroughly enjoying himself, and with that unmistakable grin across his face was making impressive speed. And contrary to all our received warnings, Friday morning was bathed in sunshine, while in Ravenna's central piazza children were leaning on the barriers, waving flags with the charismatic red arrow each time a car passed. Nearby, a nun was pushing her bicycle against the flow of cars when suddenly she stopped and produced a camera from under her habit, quickly photographed a Lancia Lambda, then walked on as if nothing had happened. Only in Italy. . .

As for the route, the Adriatic coast road is flat and fast. Louis Klemantaski - the famous photographer who accompanied Peter Collins in a works Ferrari in 1957 - has said that '180mph was achieved and held for periods of time' in that area. This year 'Klem' was back in the very same 335S Ferrari, shared this time with Peter Sachs. His quote sprang to mind as the Ferrari howled past a roadside bar that had already become host to an Aston Martin DB3, two Mercedes-Benz 300SLs and a Maserati 300S, while their crews broke for refreshment. And it is this mingling of fabulous sports racing and vintage cars with the normal goings-on and everyday traffic, which is part of the magic of the Mille Miglia. Where else could you pull up at traffic-lights behind a three-wheel scooter pick-up which is standing alongside a Ferrari 750 Monza? Or chase a 300 SLR with Jochen Mass at the wheel all the way up the crowded hill to San Marino?

Mention must be made, too, of Don Orosco's Scarab, its bright blue paint and booming exhaust proving sensational wherever it went - an aural delight in the mountains and an instantly recognisable counterpoint to the sea of red cars everywhere.

When the Mille Miglia was a real race, legend said that he who led in Rome would not win in Brescia. Maybe that reflected the fact that the run back up the western side of Italy, from Rome, via the Futa and Raticosa passes, is perhaps the most gruelling leg of all - and nowadays with more time allowed to cover it. For us, at least the dry weather continued, perhaps contributing to the relative lack of serious incident and causing some observers to suggest that this was the 'Mille Miglia del bel tempo'.

What it no longer is, officially, is a race. Back in Brescia, to help resolve the results of the regularity sections, a handicap system has been devised by the organisers, using a series of coefficients which take into account the date of design of each car plus other technical characteristics. Officially, 338 cars were entered, 329 started (the oldest a 1922 Brescia Bugatti), 84 retired and 245 finished. Most people reckon the system tends to favour the older, pre-war cars and in fact, the event was 'won', for the third time, by Giuliano Cané, partnered by Lucia Galliani in the 1937 BMW 328 Mille Miglia from the BMW Museum in Munich. In second place, 1168 points behind the winner's 9116, was the 1926 Bugatti T35C of Guasti and Bazzi, followed home in third place by the first of the post-war cars, a 1955 Ermini 375 Sport crewed by Paoletti and Specchia. But in all honesty, the result is a minor element in the Mille Miglia magic.

Next year is the fortieth anniversary of the final running of the original event, in 1957; as such, it is potentially the biggest and best 'retrospective' yet. It's a long way to go, but southern Italy in May really is a wonderful place to be.

After the war, newcomer Ferrari took over Alfa's traditional crown as dominant marque, until 1957 finale

Racing cars were simpler in Mille Miglia's day. Maserati 300S of Mozart and Moorhead came all the way from USA, didn't finish

*Louis Klemantaski returned
this year in the very same 335S
Ferrari he shared with Peter
Collins in 1957 - this time with
Peter Sachs. The Scarab follows*

*Who leads in Rome never wins
the race. Flack and McCann's
1926 Speed Six Bentley came
from USA and neither led nor
won, but did take 125th place*

Chopard

GENÈVE

depuis 1860

**« Mille Miglia »
The sporting spirit by Chopard**

Chopard at the Mille Miglia: Jacky Ickx and K-F. Scheufele

Modèle déposé **K&K** ©

Last year's champion found his 1996 season delayed by fuel vaporisation problems in the superb ex-Jackie Stewart Grand Prix Tyrrell 005

Mike Littlewood romped to first victory in his new Williams FW07B, left. Geoff Farmer in the ex-Bellof Tyrrell leads Stretton, below

DONINGTON FIA GP TROPHY 4-5 May

Early May saw the start of the season long FIA Cup series for Thoroughbred Grand Prix cars, with the opening round at Donington. The cars covered twenty years of 'recent' Grand Prix history, bringing together greats like the Lotus 72 and 78 and not so greats like the Shadow DN9s and the RAM 01. But the FIA GP racing format generally results in closer racing than you might imagine from such variously capable cars, as the range in driver talent is itself somewhat wider in historic racing than it is even in modern Formula One.

It wasn't a particularly close-run thing for the lead at the Bank Holiday meeting at Donington, though, as the combination of a very good car, John Fenning's Williams FW07B, and a very good driver, Mike Littlewood, romped away to an easy win. Littlewood had never driven the car before qualifying, but still managed to put the ex-Alan Jones Williams on pole and not surprisingly was full of praise for the car which had set the Williams team firmly on the way to the top in its heyday.

Almost instantly accustomed to his new mount, Littlewood went straight into the lead, leaving most of the race interest in the battle for second. Geordie driver Bob Berridge had qualified second in the RAM March and maintained that position. Second is where the ex-Derek Daly car would have finished too, but the extreme exertion needed to keep it ahead of more fancied cars resulted in a blown engine with only two laps left.

Martin Stretton seems to be able to drive anything old at remarkable speed but he was handicapped by fuel vaporisation before storming through the field in Jackie Stewart's old Tyrrell 005. He soon joined the six-way struggle for third (before Berridge's blow up) and set about seriously harrassing Steve Hitchins in the younger Lotus 78. In the end, though, concentration and slightly more modern technology were just enough, this time at least, to hold off a frustrated Stretton.

TROPHEE DES ARDENNES 10-12 May

This year's Trophee des Ardennes helped to celebrate Spa Francorchamp's 75th birthday, with cars almost as old as the circuit itself on hand for the occasion - but inevitably around the wide open spaces of Spa the main focus was on those cars powerful and fast enough to make the Ardennes circuit come alive. Cars like Charlie Agg's two McLaren M8Fs fit the bill perfectly.

Saturday's round of the International Supersports Cup was run in the dry, and Peter Hannen used it to extend his winning streak, having won twice at Monza. To no one's suprise it was wet on the Sunday, but Hannen's concentration and bravery didn't waver and he won again, as on Saturday ahead of Charlie Agg, but this time by a huge margin of almost half a minute, Agg simply being relieved that both his cars had stayed on the track.

Richard Evans, making his debut on the circuit, also celebrated a Spa double, winning both rounds of his own class in a 2-litre Chevron B26 which was fast enough to finish fourth overall on the Saturday and third in the wet the following day.

Heavy metal sports cars were to the fore in the weekend's two Group 4 races, with Jonathan Baker winning both legs in his Lola T70, ahead of Colin Parry-Williams' Lola T70 Spyder on both days. It was exciting stuff, and Sunday's winning margin was a mere half second, after Baker had pitted and rejoined.

The European Historic F2 Championship also had two rounds, the first of which featured an intense, race-long challenge from John Harper's March 712 which nonetheless wasn't quite enough to overcome Fredy Kumshick's Lotus 69, clinging on all of 0.22 seconds ahead at the finish. Sundays' rain, however, worked in Harper's favour, his black March this time taking the lead just two laps from home, ahead of Chris Alford's Tecno.

This was the ninth annual Trophee and it featured a win on his home circuit for Francois d'Huart in his 1950s Talbot Lago (curiously running in the prewar event) ahead of Kirk Rylands' HWM and Peter Mann's ERA AJM1. It was a popular enough win but the result just might have been different. Had Martin Morris and Sir John Venables-Llewelyn not decided to share Morris' ERA, that would almost certainly have taken the honours, but you can't share a drive without making a pit stop. . .

John Starkey's Drogo-bodied Ferrari 250GT, above, was given its debut at Spa. Chris Chiles' March 717 couldn't match the M8Fs

The Pilkingtons were out in force at Spa, including Trisha driving the Alfa Monza in the Pre-War event this time

Kirk Rylands' HWM Jaguar rounds La Source on its way to second place in the Pre-War race

24-26 MAY
Norwich Union RAC

The sheer statistics of the Norwich Union RAC Classic beggar belief. Even the first running was impressive. Back in 1986, 450 cars turned out - and from then on, it's gone from strength to strength. Ten years on, it's quadrupled in size, to make it the largest annual motoring event in the world. That means almost 1800 participants and 112 different marques, with Jaguar to the fore this year with 257, ahead of 242 MGs, 167 Triumphs and 134 Austin Healeys. And at the other end of the scale there were single representatives from some of motoring's forgotten makes, including Adler and Albion, Bayard and Belsize, Ogle and Owen, Paramount and Piper, even Vinot & Deguingand.

To crew that array of vehicles, drivers came from eight different countries, with the French easily leading the way after the British. Not exactly what you'd expect, but the explanation was that this year the Norwich Union had gone continental.

So many cars and drivers require a large number of starting points and routes, and this year, starting from eight in the morning, some 56 cars left the Trocadero Gardens in Paris, overlooked by the Eiffel Tower. From there, their schedule fitted in visits to two museums and the old Rouen les Essarts race circuit. By 11pm they were on the night boat from Le Havre to Portsmouth.

The distance the lucky crews from Paris travelled was more than matched by the Irish entries, who started from St Stephen's Green in Dublin on the Friday. After taking in Malahide Castle, the Mondello Park circuit and the Irish stud at Kildare, and after a drive through the Wicklow Mountains, they found themselves back in Dublin for an overnight stop at Dublin Castle. Saturday saw them on the ferry to Holyhead.

In complete contrast to that marathon run for the Irish, the forty cars in the Edwardian and 1920s group were given an understandably easier schedule. Starting from Silverstone they pottered along to the Heritage Motor Centre at Gaydon and then to Broughton Castle near Banbury before returning to Silverstone for the afternoon, a distance of 85 miles in all.

Where you start dictates what you see. The French starters had the best deal as their Classic lasted two days rather than the normal one, and they covered a far greater distance than all but the Irish, at around 325 miles. That contrasted sharply with the Luton entry of 123 Vauxhalls, which left the Vauxhall Heritage

The Rob Woolford/Jan Woolford 1931 Bentley, left, was one of the contingent of 177 cars which started out from Brooklands. The Ferrari Dinos congregated en masse once they had reached Silverstone

The RAC Norwich Union Classic is not a race, but some cars and drivers were clearly keener to get to Silverstone than others were

The two 1955 Swallow Dorettis were both entered by Duncan Rabagliati and, starting from Brooklands, toured what's left of the old banking

Daimlers were particularly well represented on this year's run, with 44 turning out in all and a good percentage of those were the V8 SP250s

Peter Heather and his 1959 Chevrolet Corvette, left, set off from Bath and visited Castle Combe and Prescott before reaching Silverstone. The forty intrepid Edwardians included T W Dunstall's 1911 Delahaye Type 43, right

Centre and called at Duxford airfield to see the Imperial War Museum's display, next to Wimpole Hall and then to Millbrook and the impressive test circuit before getting to the Silverstone Grand Prix circuit from 1.30 onwards, for an afternoon of varied if somewhat damp events.

Over 300 cars left the Bath start by different roads, en route to Castle Combe and Prescott, perhaps to give some of the drivers from April's Haynes RAC event a touch of déja vù. Some went from there to Gaydon's Heritage Motor Centre. Every one of the dozen routes provided a varied morning's driving and sights. Cheltenham's 180 cars also got to experience Prescott, and then the Lucas test track at Fern End, Kenilworth, followed by the Jaguar Museum at Coventry.

Starters from Brooklands had the pleasure of seeing how Britain's oldest circuit is reviving. The track has long since disappeared and the remaining banking will never be repaired, but the Club House and the 'Sheds', where the likes of Malcolm Campbell's racing cars were prepared, are perfectly restored.

Brooklands is a day out in itself but the cars had other appointments to keep, at Longcross military proving grounds where the circuit has its own small banked sections, albeit rather smaller than Brooklands'. Another test track, at Crowthorne, was next up and the other highlight was the Aston Martin factory at Newport Pagnell.

The 76 cars which left Shrewsbury combined sights as varied as the Bass Museum at Burton on Trent, the Motor Industry Research Association's test track at Nuneaton and the Sir Henry Royce Memorial Trust at Paulerspury. All routes ended at Silverstone, where the cars lapped the circuit and took part in autotests, while some of the drivers took part in the Best Dressed competition. The one sting in the tail, as anyone who has driven to the British Grand Prix knows, is that getting into the circuit can take an age. It did this time too, and the problem was made worse by the main entrance being closed for some reason. With the day's weather turning wet and miserable, the last thing anyone wanted at this stage was to sit in a dripping traffic jam.

An event the size of the Norwich Union clearly needs almost military levels of organisation and this was an unusual and unfortunate lapse which suggested that maybe the event has finally grown just too big, a victim of its own enormous success. That may be possible, but it would still be a shame for an 'everyone welcome' event (well every car over twenty years old anyway) to be forced to limit its numbers. May it never be necessary.

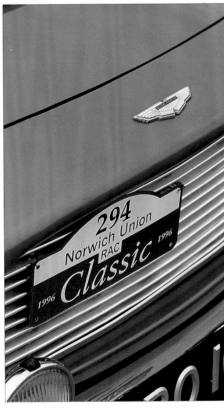

Clive Godfrey's Austin Healey 3000, above. The one thing that could have been better for the 1996 Norwich Union, apart from the access to the Silverstone GP circuit, was the weather. But that was unfortunately outside the organisers' control

Race circuit sections encouraged bursts of enthusiastic hooliganism among an exotic mix of cars such as Alfa GT Junior Zagato and Alpine A110. Porsche crew seek escape route

The Coupe des Alpes, for all its famous name, surely had some of the wackiest racers of the year, and high among those was what is presumably a GT40 lookalike

The Lancia Stratos was a kit car even when it was genuine, using Ferrari, Lancia and Fiat parts bins to create one of the ultimate homologation specials

Caterham Seven driver discovers the edge of adhesion in the foothills, left. Swiss Healey Silverstone is pursued by XK140 through lunar landscape with snow, right

Chris Rea's look says it all as he sits in a vision that became reality

Chris Rea

*Fuelled by a passion for Ferrari, and Wolfgang
von Trips' car in particular, musician Chris Rea
has produced a sharknose 156 where before there
were only photographs and faded memories.
PETER TOMALIN takes up the story*

When Chris Rea's Dino 156 was wheeled out
at Goodwood in 1995, it was the first time
anyone had seen a 'sharknose' Ferrari F1
car in the metal since 1962. These days,
when even small parts of racing cars are
stashed away as investments, it seems incredible that Ferrari, as a
matter of course, used to scrap its Grand Prix cars once they'd
finished their 'useful' life. From 1956 to 1962, all those prancing
horses were carted off to the knacker's yard, dismantled and most
parts crushed. So this 156 is a replica because it couldn't be anything else - or rather it is a meticulous recreation of a small piece
of motoring history, made possible by a very driven man.

Chris Rea is passionate, some might say obsessive, about
Ferrari. In 1996 we saw the conclusive proof of his passion with
the release of his first ever feature film called, logically enough, La
Passione. It's the story of a lad called Jo, growing up in Scotland,
the son of an immigrant Italian ice-cream maker, who becomes
obsessed with Ferrari. Specifically, he becomes obsessed with the
Scuderia driver Wolfgang Von Trips, the German ace killed while
driving a 'sharknose' in 1961 - when he was perhaps only two
races away from the world championship. The film shows how
Jo's obsession leads him to Italy, via a series of dream sequences.

Chris Rea was that boy. His Italian father, who sold ice
cream from a shop in Middlesboro, planted the seeds of his passion when Chris was growing up in the late 1950s and early '60s.

*Could you
detect the
difference?
Even racing
historians
are hard
pushed to be
critical, so
faithfully
have Chris
Rea and his
small team
crafted their
homage to
von Trips'
Ferrari*

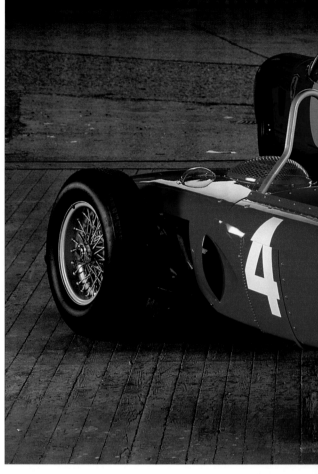

It's Aintree in 1961, with von Trips in the sharknose, left. Soon after, he would be killed in the car at Monza. Behind the Formula One car, right, is the replica Le Mans Ferrari 250TR/61 built for Rea's film La Passione

'On family holidays, when we'd drive down to Italy, the route would be carefully planned to take in Silverstone and Brands Hatch, and we'd stop over in Reims', he recalls, in his gruff Geordie-via-Marlboro-country drawl. 'Then my father would wax lyrical about Ferraris, these blood-red cars that were faster than any other. It was almost like a religion'.

It was the summer of 1961, and the day of the French Grand Prix at Reims when Rea saw the light. Watching the race on TV in the family home above the shop, his imagination was fired by Giancarlo Baghetti's inspired drive in the 156, taking the flag in his very first Grand Prix. 'Everything about that day was glorious', says Rea, 'and that was it. Instant passion'.

It was another Ferrari driver, though, who really gripped the young Rea's imagination. 'There was this strange baron from Germany, who the writers said had a real wild touch to his driving, and he was driving this blood-red car that was faster than any other. He became an almost mystical figure to me'.

Wolfgang von Trips was leading the drivers' championship when at Monza later that same season his 156 collided with Jim Clark's Lotus and somersaulted off the track, killing von Trips and several of the crowd. 'That was my first ever experience of death', says Rea. 'It has lived with me ever since. . .'

His life-long fascination with von Trips and the sharknose Ferrari bore real fruit with the replica 156 which he commissioned to star in La Passione. Both were labours of love. The film, which stars Paul Shane, Carmen Silvera, Keith Barron, and Sean Gallagher as Jo, was written and produced by Rea, as was all the music. And that car. The 156, built by Shoreham-based engineer Paul Harvey around a faithfully reproduced spaceframe and a distantly related V6 from the pretty, late-1960s Dino 206 road car, caused quite a stir when it was revealed at the 1995 Goodwood Festival of Speed where 1961 world champion Phil Hill drove it to give it an unofficial seal of approval.

Filming for La Passione started soon after that and took five months in all, with location work in Germany, Italy and, of course, at Reims. Rea explains how it all came about. 'It started around four years ago', he says. 'When I had some down-time in the studio. I thought I'd make a video, a collage of Ferrari history, but the idea developed. . .' Eventually it became the story of a boy who goes off to make his fortune, to buy a Ferrari, by stealing the family vanilla ice-cream recipe and turning it into a world beating perfume. And he chases this ghost of Wolfgang. . .'

For one of the film props, Rea had a replica Ferrari sports car, visually similar to the 1961 Le Mans-winning 250TR/61,

At Goodwood circuit Chris Rea must have felt in a time warp, with his 156 alongside Ferrari world champion Phil Hill in this (genuine) 1960 Ferrari Dino 246 F1 car

built around a cut-down 330GTC which he himself used to race. But when it came to the Formula 1 car, obsession took over. The further he got into it, the more he wanted to build a faithful replica, and that was when he turned to Paul Harvey.

The 156F1, unveiled in 1961 and Ferrari's first rear-engined racing car, was an all-time great. It looked dramatic with its characteristic nostrils, which designer Fantuzzi reckoned to be more aerodynamic than a single slot. It was powered by one of two new engines: both 1.5 litre V6s, but one with a 65 degree angle between banks, the other 120 degrees, the latter developing a grid-leading 190bhp. In 1961 it was virtually unbeatable.

'When people found out I was planning to build a replica, they told me to tread carefully, that I was on sacred ground', says Rea. 'And Paul thought there was more to them than there actually was. But I kept showing him a picture of Mairesse's overturned car, revealing the chassis, which looked a bit like the box-frames we used to use for lighting rigs on tour! Once we became less frightened of treading on holy ground, we just went for it.

'This is no longer just a film prop. It's as close as we could get to the original. The difficult thing was the body. We had quite a lot of photos, but there were 17 different shapes to the tops, because they were all hand beaten. I had to tell them the first body just wasn't right. Remember, I'd had a picture of this car on my wall nearly all my life. It's terrible, when you're obsessed. . . In the end I said, 'Just imagine you're having to do it in time for a race.' It was the Italian thing: singing, drinking wine, hammering away. . .'

The most soul-searching surrounded the engine. Paul Harvey eventually found a 1967 206 Dino engine. 'It's a relative of the original,' says Harvey, 'but we had to dry sump it, and throw the ignition system away because that stuck out so far it would have been in the driver's right shoulder. But it makes a similar noise and it produces 180bhp from 2 litres - about the same as the 1.5-litre race engine.

'Ferrari were unable to help with any original drawings - they may have gone the same way as the cars - but we had about six dimensions, including wheelbase and track, and we made up a dummy frame so we could position the wheels, driveshafts and so on. Once we'd got the proportions right, the engine and drive-train virtually slotted into place, and that gave us confidence'.

When the car was near complete, after around 2000 hours work, Rea and Harvey invited F1 guru Nigel Roebuck and racing historian Doug Nye to private viewings. 'When Roebuck and Nye didn't laugh, I thought we'd probably got there', smiles Rea.

And Nye, author of 'Dino, the little Ferrari', recalls: 'I was in two minds, because I wasn't sure how I was going to handle it if it had been a disaster. But Paul rolled up the garage door and there was this nostril nose. What struck me was the side of the car, with those big dome-head rivets. I thought 'The bloody thing looks real.' It was extraordinary, like photographs come to life'.

Rea adds: I'd have loved to have walked in like Doug did, never having seen it before. It's a bit like song writing - you get too close to it. You see it when it's four wheels, and then with the tub, and then with a steering wheel. And there were times when you had to bite the bullet and say no, let's re-do that. But now, thank God, just looking at it proves it all worthwhile'.

The replica 250 Testa Rossa, top, was inspired by the 1961 Le Mans winning car and based on a cut-down 330GTC. The lines of the sharknose, above, have been perfectly reproduced, working from nothing much more than old photographs

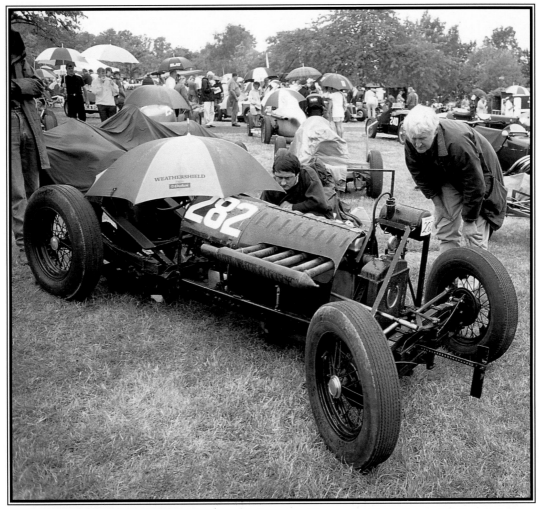

It may officially have been summer but the umbrellas were still out at the VSCC's Prescott hillclimb in July

SUMMER

From July to September, the summer scene is packed with races and events, from hillclimbs at Prescott and Shelsley Walsh, to races at Donington and Silverstone, not to mention classic car runs across every country in western Europe and concours for the world's most elegant cars

13 July

Walter 'Wally' Hassan died at the age of 91. He had packed a huge amount into those years. He had no inclination to follow his father's footsteps into gentleman's outfitting and started with Bentley as employee number 15. He went on to take charge of Bentley's racing team, worked for ERA and BRM man Raymond Mays, and then at Thompson & Taylor at Brooklands, where he helped build John Cobb's Napier Railton. His career spanned many eras as he went on to join Jaguar and worked with Bill Heynes on developing the XK twin-cam. Years later, after helping to turn the famous Coventry Climax fire pump engine into a championship winning F1 engine, he found himself once more collaborating to make one of the world's great engines, the Jaguar V12.

26 July

Prince Michael of Kent invited the Brooklands Society to organise a centennial display of the British motor industry's finest, at Ascot for the Queen's Charity Race Day and 100 cars turned up, ranging from an 1896 Daimler to a 1996 Aston DB7. Even Bentley Old No 1 was there, having spent the last six years in storage.

27-28 July

The VSCC went hillclimbing at Prescott and Mark Walker took his Parker GN Special up the tricky hill faster than anyone to set a new Vintage course record in 41.79 seconds.

2-4 August

At the annual auction at the Coys Festival the Ferrari 166 Spider Corsa stayed unsold after bidding stopped at £270,000. How things have changed. But away from the auction in one of the many stalls you could find the steering wheel from Niki Lauda's near fatal crash in his Ferrari at the Nurburgring. Suitably bent and twisted it sold for £2000. How many more are waiting on the assembly line for future shows though? The Chrysler-sponsored Coys Festival helped Sir Jack Brabham celebrate his 70th birthday. Sir Jack drove his championship winning BT19, son David the Tasman BT7A, Tim Schenken drove the lobster claw BT34 and Ron Tauranac managed to spin twice in the BT4.

3-4 August

The 22nd European Historic GP at Zolder saw the usual mix of Alfas, TVRs, Healeys and Porsches but shining bright above all those was a Silver Arrow, a Mercedes W154 (opposite page), giving a demonstration run around the GP circuit

16-18 August

Showing there's still plenty of money in California at Pebble Beach Christie's sold a Ferrari 166M for $1,625,000 when it was expected only to reach a million dollars. On the same weekend the record breaking Mormon Meteors were reunited. Few onlookers could have believed that Ab Jenkins drove one of them at 195mph for a whole hour.

25 August

The longest running sponsorship deal in Formula 1 came to an end as Marlboro left McLaren after 23 mostly very successful years dating back to the days of the M23s of former world champions Denny Hulme and Emerson Fittipaldi

7-8 September

The Parc Bagatelle concours in Paris went the same way as the Villa d'Este earlier in the year, with the

John Mozart's wonderful Alfa Romeo 8C 2900B won best of show at the Bagatelle Concours in Paris in September

best of show award going to an open Alfa Romeo 8C 2900B. Other Alfas on show included the Donington Collection's frightening Bimotore.

7-8 September
Christie's auctioned one of the more bizarre car collections of recent times. Alexander Miller of Vermont was obsessed by Stutz cars and had 32 of them dotted around his estate in various states of disrepair. Miller was a true eccentric, an autogiro pilot and believer in gold bullion, a considerable amount of which was also discovered along with the decaying Stutzs. Despite the condition of most of the cars, their prices were way beyond the estimates, fetching £1.3 million in all with one Bearcat making £110,000

8 September
Now in its tenth year, the annual Chicago British Car Festival at Des Plaines Illinois, attracted over 700 British cars - to show that interest in British cars still burns faintly in at least some American breasts.

13-15 September
Brighton Football Club might well be on the brink of extinction but the annual Speed Trials show no signs of fading away and David Baldock's Alta was the fastest vintage car on show, rocketing along the seafront in 13.24 seconds.

28-29 September
The sunshine of the Coys Festival was long gone when the cars returned to the Silverstone circuit in late September, although the good season the Aston Martin DBR1 has been having continued, this time with Paul Hardiman bringing it home for another first place.

29 September
The VSCC's Richard Seaman Memorial meeting at Donington was the third in a row at which Tim Llewellyn has won the vintage trophy, and the seventh in all.. His 8.4-litre Bentley finished ahead of Robin Baker's 27-litre Hispano-engined Delage. Ludovic Lindsay won the Richard Seaman Trophy for pre-war cars in his ERA, Remus.

A driver change for the Richard Attwood/Gary Pearson Lister Jaguar, which went on to win the Groveair race with ease

Ludwig Willisch's smart Cooper T45 ducks neatly inside Terry Cohn's 1932 Alfa Monza, right. Hall (12) and Harper (2) battled hard in the European Historic F2 race with Hall coming out on top

DONINGTON SUPERPRIX 1-2 June

As would be demonstrated in a different context at Spa later in the year, there are times when in spite of a full programme and all the right cars, the crowds inexplicably fail to materialise on the day. And again as at Spa, those who stayed away from Donington in early June missed a treat in the Superprix meeting.

The main event here was the Donington Cup for Historic GP cars, and Rod Jolley in his Cooper T51 and Philip Walker in the Lotus 16 were clearly the pick of the field. In fact the pair had been so quick in practice that they agreed to start from the pit lane - yet even with that handicap it was only seven laps before they had stormed past Burkhard von Schenk's Maserati 250F and started swapping the lead between themselves.

The race then appeared to be Walker's, after he had recovered from a quick spin and retaken the lead going into Redgate on the last lap, but Jolley had other ideas and pounced between the chicane and the flag, to win by a matter of feet.

Entertaining though Walker and Jolley's Donington Cup battle was, the two rounds of the European Historic F2 championship were more competitive across the field. By the end of the first lap, hampered by a temporary misfire, pole position man Rob Hall had been swallowed up by the pack and was back in eighth place. But six laps later he forced his March 712 past Bob Juggins' Lola 240 into second place and a lap later John Harper's March 712 was swallowed up too and Hall led to the finish.

In the second round, on Sunday, Hall won again, but had to fight pretty hard for it. This time he made no mistake at the start but he never did shake off Harper, who dogged him for the whole race. Third again was Fredy Kumschick in the Lotus 69, producing a repeat of his Saturday result.

John Harper and Philip Walker were both out again in the pre-1965 F1 challenge, similarly mounted in Tasman Brabhams - Harper's a BT4 and Walker's a BT7A. Walker just held off

Harper but, behind them, the star of the show was Richard Attwood in a Cooper T51 who had cut his way through most of the field before his car expired just as he was preparing to dispute third place with Alan Baillie's BT14.

Between races, the historic GP theme was underlined with a tribute to BRM's past glories, which included Donington's V16 in shrill action driven by Rick Hall, and Tom Wheatcroft in his P25, with such famous BRM names as Louis Stanley and Tony Rudd looking on. It wasn't all single seaters at Donington, though, and the weekend's 15 races included the Groveair Endurance Challenge which started at 5pm on the Saturday, just as some of the crowd was already making tracks home.

John Harper continued his busy weekend in the Groveair race, and his Cooper Monaco held second place to Gary Pearson's Lister Jaguar for a spell before pitting and retiring. Tony Smith's Maserati Birdcage also led for ten laps around half distance until something broke in its valve train, by which time Pearson had handed over to Richard Attwood who held off Peter Hannen in the Cooper Monaco. Hannen might have challenged harder had the Cooper's engine been running more strongly, but in the end, Attwood's enormous experience and a level of skill which has been little diminished by the years were enough to win it.

Of the other races, a classic Lola/Chevron battle in the Group 4 event was resolved in Chevron's favour, with Kent Abrahamsson's B16 ahead of Jonathan Baker's bigger Lola T70 and Ivan Mahe's T70 third, but some way back. And finally, the historic saloon victory went to Ted Williams as his Mustang overhauled Nevil Smith's Lotus Cortina, while the big Healeys also looked very much at home at Donington in the Austin Healey Challenge. In the Healeys as in the Donington Cup, the lead battle was resolved after the chicane on the last lap, in this case with Dennis Welch taking advantage of Bruce Montgomery's error to add his name to the weekend winner's list.

To the delight of the small but enthusiastic crowd, the Donington Museum's own screaming BRM V16 was given a demonstration outing by Rick Hall

Ian Nuttall's 1952 Alta being left in the wake of Rod Jolley's Cooper T51 and Phil Walker's Lotus 16, right. John Harper's Brabham BT4, below, finished a close second in the Pre-65 F1 Challenge

Original

1896 ARNOLD

Our Hall of Fame has many fine examples of cars from
the dawn of motoring including an 1899 Renault,
believed to be the oldest in existence, and the
1896 Arnold that took a place in the original Londo
to Brighton Emancipation run

Historic

RECORD BREAKING BLUEBIRD

World Record Breakers like Bluebird and Golden
Arrow, Formula One cars driven by Prost, Senna and
other past racing Champions plus many early
examples of legendary cars such as the 'Mini' can be
viewed in a superb collection of more than
250 vehicles.

Beautiful

JAGUAR XJ 220

So, whether you enjoy the beauty of vintage, veteran or
classic cars, or the sleek lines of sports cars through
the ages, there is no better place to see them.

Beaulieu

In the Heart of the New Forest

NATIONAL MOTOR MUSEUM • PALACE HOUSE & GARDENS
ABBEY AND EXHIBITION • RIDES AND DRIVES.

Open daily from 10am except Christmas Day. For further information call (01590) 612123 (24hrs) or (01590) 612345
John Montagu Building, Beaulieu, Brockenhurst, Hants. SO42 7ZN.

All main attractions and facilities open daily throughout the year. Operating times for some features vary by season. Check for details if you wish. Times of operation on day of visit are displayed on arrival.

GIRO DI SICILIA 4-8 June

Sadly, given its promising location and a very decent entry, the eighth Giro di Sicilia, or Tour of Sicily if you prefer the less romantic English version, was tarnished by complaints even before the start, and by arguments at the finish, even during the prize giving ceremony itself.

The early moans were over the fact that the Giro's date had to be swapped from April to June because of local elections, and that had made finding hotel accommodation for the 110 crews a nightmare. It was a real embarassment for the organisers, the Panormus Veteran Car Club, with guests of honour on the entry list including the likes of the President of the ASI, driving a superb Lancia D24, and the President of Nissan Italy, Greco Musumeci, in a Datsun 240Z.

Then, even in June, the weather gave the teams something else to worry about. The first leg, from Palermo to Trapani in the far north west end of the island, although only 80km as the crow flies, was held at night during a huge storm. Those driving open cars soon had water on both sides of the 'screen to contend with, and couldn't see a thing. Luckily the sun came out for the second leg, the 217km from Trapani to Sciacca all along the eastern coast of Sicily, passing the saltworks at Marsala and the beauty of Erice. From Sciacca it was on to Catania along the south coast via Gela and Agrigento, before branching inland to Comiso and Ragusa.

So far everything had gone perfectly; one of the many time checks was at Ragusa Ibla, so that crews were forced to stop and admire the mountain scenery and the day ended at Villa Bernini at 4.30, leaving a very civilised interval before dinner and the overnight halt. Nothing could have been more agreeable.

But after a while it becomes obvious that there's a fundamental clash of personalities between the ultra competitive Italians and the rest. Drivers like Mazzola in the 1963 Porsche 356C and Galli in the 1953 Siata 300BC were out to win, taking it all very seriously and getting the time controls down to a fine art. Most of the others were more intent on enjoying the roads and the scenery at whatever speed they liked without the worry of driving to the accuracy of the last second. One French pair made that point perfectly; the impressive stopwatches that they wore around their necks were works of art - in cardboard.

Even with this relaxed view, disagreements turning into arguments began to sour the event, and cancelling the timecheck at Messina added to the confusion and irritation. That carried over to the prizegiving ceremony itself, spoiling the evening somewhat as the Porsche pairing of Mazzola/Cicotti took their trophy ahead of Galli/Faccenda in the Siata. Given the appeal of the previous Tours of Sicily this year's problems were probably just a one-off glitch. For the future of the event, let's hope so.

Maurizio Tabucchi's Alfa Giulietta SZ navigates its way through Torre Macauda, right at the beginning of the third leg

On day one, this Maserati, along with all the other open cars, was literally awash during the heavy storm - but, happily, the sun was out by the next day

Winner of the Women's cup was Coppia Di Lorenzo, driving the wonderful Cisitalia Colombo Corsa, and seen here on the Colli Rizzo

Some of the time controls, like this one, went like clockwork, the Daimler SP250's crew in this case quite unflustered. Some aspects were less smooth

All out to win on their home soil, the Italians were taking the Giro di Sicilia far more seriously, whatever unlikely machines they were driving

Louis Vuitton

*The 1996 Louis Vuitton Concours d'Elégance was the well established blend
of big names and glamorous cars. PETER TOMALIN joined the select
gathering on the manicured lawns of London's Hurlingham Club*

All day long, there's the gentle clack of croquet mallets against a background of genteel chat, and I can't help thinking that this is the sound of money. Wheeled art decorates the lush, clipped lawns of London's prestigious Hurlingham Club; champagne corks rocket into the June air, to the accompanying chink-chink of crystal glasses; pop stars spangle society's upper crust; and, in the evening, the ball gowns come gliding across the lawns, to ride the steam carousel, picnic by candlelight and dance into the early hours. It's life, Jim, but not as I know it.

Just occasionally, the afternoon is torn in two by the ferocious bark of a racing engine. Mechanics have been labouring to persuade a flame-red Maserati 250F into life, and when it finally lets rip, the crowd race to surround it. But it's all revved up and nowhere to go, and just for a moment the whole affair seems slightly bizarre. Later it'll pop and cough its way round the grounds - it's a condition of entry that all the cars have to be seen to be in working order, but it does seem odd for a racing car.

Still, there's something undeniably seductive about the Louis Vuitton Concours d'Elegance, and the seventh edition, held on June 1, 1996, and blessed by an appropriately English mixture of sunshine and showers, had all the right ingredients: the weather, the setting, the people - from Alan Whicker to Stirling Moss to Simon Le Bon. Oh, and the cars. The cars aren't half bad.

First to catch my eye is Tim Scott's heroic 60hp Mercédès, just like the one that carried the Belgian Jenatzy to victory in the 1903 Gordon Bennett Cup Race. I know this car from a previous life; it featured on the cover of a magazine called Superclassics, which I had the all-too-brief pleasure of editing a year or so ago. Today, with its tanks and tubes and drip-feeds, all brass and copper, all gleaming, the car looks a picture. Tim attends to some last-minute buffing. Behind the Mercédès is a glistening 1912 Rolls-Royce Silver Ghost. That's Tim's, too. He's had them both brought over from Jersey specially for the Concours. 'Well, I reckon you've got to do all these events at least once', he says. Has it been worth it? 'It's a nice day, it's a nice get-together, there are some lovely cars, the sun's shining, and in a minute I'm going to

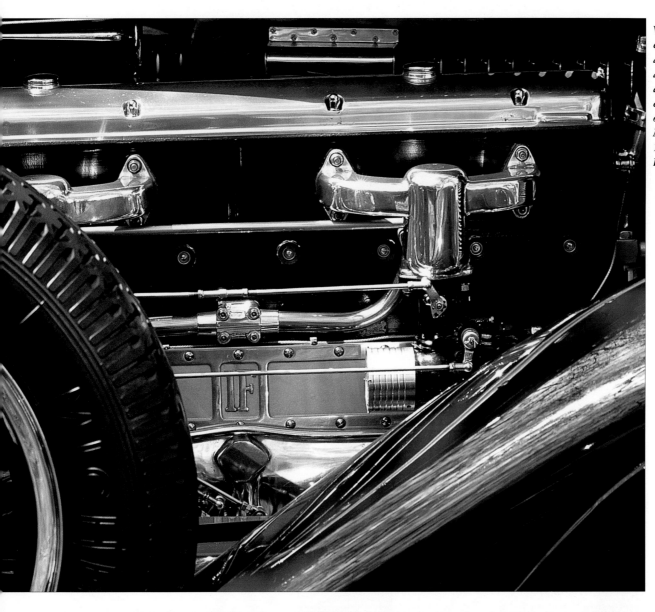

Wonderful engineering and stunning attention to detail in the engine of Best of Show winner, Mr Bill Haines' 1932 Isotta Fraschini 8B

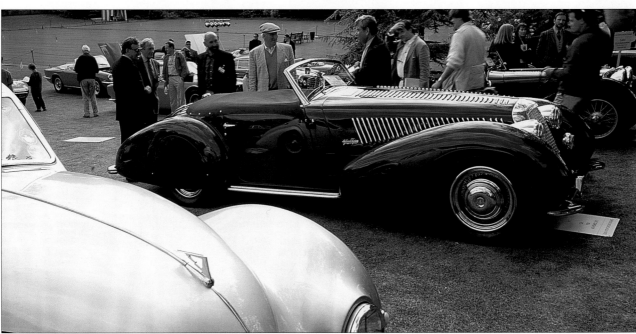

Rare outing for the Aston Martin Atom in the foreground, and Pre-War Sports Cars trophy for Mr Arturo Keller's 1938 Alfa Romeo 2.9B

have a glass of champagne. It can't be all that bad, can it. . .

What does he think the judges are looking for? 'Different judges look for different things. Originality is most important for some; for others it's style and elegance.' I take a few minutes to admire the Ghost, one of the 'London-Edinburgh' models. Its original owner was a maharajah; why am I not surprised? I am absolutely certain Tim will leave with at least one trophy.

Did I say certain? There is, I begin to realise, no shortage of spectacular entries, and what's pleasing is the variety: it's not just chrome and brass-laden glamour-wagons, but some nicely original single-seaters, and some genuinely interesting cars, like the Aston Martin 'Atom', the car which, so the story goes, convinced David Brown that Astons had a future, so thank heaven for that.

My eyes are drawn, too, to a supremely elegant Phantom III, made in 1937, with coachwork by Barker; then to a 1960 Maserati 3500 Vignale Spyder, and behind it, its race relation, the glorious 250F. There's a special class for Maserati this year, to celebrate 70 years of the marque, and I'm rather glad, because as well as these two and several other fantastic cars, it's flushed out an absolute gem. This 8CL was apparently the last car built by Maserati in 1939 before war stopped play, and according to Tony Merrick, who's been entrusted with its maintenance by new owner Peter Rae, there's still the original paint on the chassis. I have just found my favourite car of the day.

Ah, but what about the stupendous Isotta Fraschini 8B? Eight-cylinder, 7372cc engine; a chassis which cost £1900 in 1932; coachwork by Viggo Jensen; ostrich trim on the inside, and

outside a huge searchlight for. . . who knows? Shooting polar bear perhaps (this car was once driven to the Arctic Circle by Danish nobility). American Bill Haines has had it subjected to a five-year restoration, and when it was completed in August 1995, it was a first-time-out concours winner, at Pebble Beach. Where it was unanimously judged Best in Show. The words 'big fish' and 'small pond' come to mind. Still, it's a treat to see it.

Nick Mason is here both as a judge (in the Post War Touring Car class) and as an entrant, with his 1901 Panhard et Levassor. 'Unfortunately I'm not allowed to judge my own car, otherwise I think we could be in for a result', he smiles. What criteria does he use? 'Well, all the judges have guidelines. You end up looking for detail, really, to see how carefully a car's been restored. What about over-restoration? 'In Europe people are careful about the way they restore cars. There might have been an American tendency 20 years ago to chrome things that should be steel, which is silly and dangerous, but that's gone.'

And as someone who really likes to use historic cars, does he approve of concours? 'Yes' he says without hesitation. 'I don't believe that cars should only be raced. The important thing is to have a spread of events'.

It might not be everyone's cup of Veuve Clicquot, but there is a place for events like this, and the Hurlingham Club is as good a place as any. The results? The Isotta Fraschini won Best of Show, the 8CL Maser had the Rolls-Royce Trophy for engineering excellence, Tim Scott's Mercédès and his Rolls-Royce each won its class, and Charles, I believe, won the croquet. Chin-chin.

The 1903 Mercedes 60hp, above and opposite, was the racing car which founded the Mercedes dynasty and brought car design out of the Edwardian era

YOUNGTIMER NURBURGRING *14-15 June*

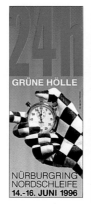

Germany's Youngtimer caters for newer classics and the 14-15 June meet was held on the same weekend as the 24-hour race on the old 'Ring, It saw everything from Opels, above left, to 911s, left, and this wonderful Fiat Abarth 1000TC, below. The grids are full with BMWs battling NSU Prinzs and Ford Escorts, right

ASTON MARTIN ST JOHN HORSFALL 9 June

There are two curiosities about the Aston Martin Owners Club's annual St John Horsfall meeting. One is the name itself, which for the unitiated is in memory of Aston driver Jock Horsfall. The other is that you see far more than just Aston Martins in action.

The meeting takes place at Silverstone on the day after the VSCC's Hawthorn Trophy event, and traditionally some of the cars and spectators stay on, in this case being entertained from the word go by the ERF Intermarque round, in which Mike Burt's Porsche 930 was always going to be a hard nut to crack.

Then, following his second place in the Marsh Plant Hire DBS V8 behind Burt's uncatchable 930 in that race, David Heynes was fated to have another frustrating second place, in the Postwar Aston Martin race, even after he had taken advantage of a bungled start from Tony Dron. At the critical moment, Dron had been looking at his water temperature gauge rather than the more crucial starting signal, which let Heynes get the drop on him. Heynes then kept the lead until just one lap from the finish, when John Freeman's charge in his Aston V8 took him past both of them - to win, by just three seconds.

Non Astons then dominated the AMOC Historic Car Championship round, where Don Orosco in the perfectly restored Scarab got confused over which was warm-up and which was race - to the extent that he finished two laps down, in spite of having been on pole for the start! Orosco's mistake left Frank Sytner, perfectly at home in the D-type as usual, to an easier than expected win, particularly as hard charging Barrie Williams cooked the clutch in his car at the start and was never in contention.

The St John Horsfall Trophy itself, for prewar Astons, had several Le Mans factory team cars among the 22 entrants. For the ten laps, and averaging over 68mph, David Freeman was in the same form that would also take him to victory in the postwar Aston race. He was simply uncatchable in the Speed Model which Jock Horsfall himself drove to fourth place in the Spa 24 Hours in 1949. Freeman finished just over three seconds ahead of Andy Bell, with Nick Mason back in third. His performance, even so, wasn't enough to win the trophy - with the machinations of the race's handicap system giving it to Chloe Mason.

Simon Draper's DB3S leads Chloe Mason, who was to win the St John Horsfall Trophy for pre-war Astons

John Goldsmith gets it wrong as Ed Sharpe in his 1959 DB4 cuts inside the sliding DB6

David Clark's Lister crowds onto Barrie Williams' Tojeiro, right. Don Orosco had a fraught time in the Scarab, below, confusing warm-up laps and race laps

The Italian entries included these two Alfa Romeo 6C 2500s, seen here pausing in Stratford, the front one a Touring-bodied coupe

You could not celebrate the centenary of the British motor industry without the erstwhile Best Car in the World. Germany's rival for that title was there in force, too, with some superb cars, including this Mercedes 500K, below

FIVA WORLD RALLY 14-23 *June*

Mention the FIVA World Rally even to keen classic car enthusiasts and you are likely to be met with blank looks. It took place, all went well and everyone had a jolly good time - but the big event still appeared to be a well kept secret.

The FIVA World Rally is a movable feast. Every year the Federation Internationale des Vehicules Anciens associates itself with a large classic car event somewhere in the world - and this year, reasonably enough given the centenary, it was Britain. From 21 countries, over 300 vehicles turned up for day one at Holyrood Park, Edinburgh. The oldest hadn't needed to travel far; the Heritage Trust's 1896 Wolseley Trike's journey was only from Coventry - to where, again reasonably enough, the Rally would return almost ten days later.

And if the oldest human entrants couldn't match the Wolseley's 19th century origins, at least the twin Eastwood brothers did celebrate their 80th birthdays during the Rally - although, unfortunately, their 1915 Olds ended its run after an accident in York. A Japanese crewed Mini was more fortunate. It collided with a bridge but was patched up and kept going.

Those who had stumped up their £1800 entry fee and travelled from the ends of the earth were rewarded with perfect weather and a route which made the best of it. From Edinburgh it headed north as far as Lochearnhead, back south around the Borders, through the Lake District (with a diverting reception on steam boats on Lake Windermere), down to Donington, Stratford and finally back to Gaydon in the heart of British motor industry land - although some had far longer jaunts in mind, and from Gaydon, the intrepid Noel McIntosh almost immediately set off again in his 1913 Vauxhall D type, destination Australia, via Russia and Mongolia.

There were regularity sections, and speed checks once in a while, along with driving tests, at the motor industry proving grounds at MIRA for example; but although the competitive element was fairly undemanding, there was in theory an overall winner in the form of the Revington/Revington Triumph TR4 which also won the Mintex Cup along the way - and that was just one of no fewer than thirty different prizes and awards.

FORD AT LE MANS 15 *June*

Thirty years ago, Ford scored the first of four consecutive Le Mans victories, winning, as Le Mans tradition dictated, at the third attempt. For two years, the GT40s had threatened to achieve Ford's ambition of beating Ferrari. In 1966, with the arrival of the latest 7-litre cars, they did it - and did it with a vengeance.

At half distance GT40s held the first six positions, and as the end of the race approached with the two leading cars of Bruce McLaren/Chris Amon and Ken Miles/Denny Hulme on the same lap, Ford hatched thoughts of staging the first Le Mans dead heat.

In the final laps, pit signals slowed the John Miles car, which was leading at the time, to allow McLaren to form up for a formation finish - with the third placed GT40 behind.

They did finish virtually side by side as the flag fell, but the organisers declared that because McLaren and Amon had started further down the grid, they had covered a greater distance and they were the winners. So instead of 1-1-3, it was merely 1-2-3.

This year the three actual cars involved in the 1966 finish came back to Le Mans to recreate it. All three, now immaculately restored and virtually indistinguishable from how they looked on the day, thirty years ago, were brought from America by Lufthansa. They were driven by their current owners, George Stauffer, Bryan Mimaki and Ken Quintenz, and a little piece of Le Mans history brought back a lot of memories.

One look confirmed the worst: Sean Treacey's Lancia, left, had broken a drive-shaft. This retirement helped elevate the flying TR4, below, of Michael Stevenson, into a well deserved second place

DONEGAL RALLY 22-23 *June*

Cathal Curley, winner of the first Donegal Rally 25 years ago, was dragged kicking and screaming out of retirement to celebrate the rally's Silver Jubilee, driving Beatty Crawford's 911.

John Keatley was on the boil from the very first stage, to pull out a slender lead from Dessie Nutt and John Coyne, while Niall Creighton in the Lotus Cortina was having his own battle with Alan Courtney and the Lancia Fulvia HF of Sean Treacey - but his rally ended when a driveshaft broke on the second day, losing him a certain third place. Treacey fared little better, as his Fulvia broke its exhaust manifold, and allowed the ever improving Michael Stevenson to bring his TR4 home in second place.

Cathal Curley had taken a while to get used to the left-hand drive 911. Perhaps he should have taken longer still, as he now started to dent it stage by stage, leaving its owner to remark 'I wish he would keep it more on the black stuff. . .'

Curley clearly didn't hear that though, and on the last stage really excelled himself. He was a joy to watch, but then on a fast left after a downhill section, thousands of TV viewers saw the Porsche understeer to the right, demolishing a long, long row of fence posts before nosediving into the river. Cathal will not be finding a place on Beatty's Christmas card list this year. And that left an overjoyed Dessie Nutt to mount the winner's ramp in Letterkenny, putting his recent bad luck behind him.

Suspension on full droop, the Hillman Hunter of Ernest Stewart and Jerry Carr flies in pursuit of the distant leaders

With Cathal Curley throwing his Porsche 911 into the river, there was nothing to stop Dessie Nutt and Derek Smith taking the win in the familiar bright yellow 911

Geoff Farmer took pole position at the Nurburgring and came home third in the ex-Bellof Tyrrell

Michael Schryver, left, was fifth in Germany in one of the older cars, the ex-Wissell Lotus 72, left. Mike Wrigley's Shadow DN9, below, fought for second place at Anderstorp

FIA CUP NURBURGRING *June 12*

From Donington the FIA Cup had moved to Magny Cours where John Fenning's Williams FW07 held off Steve Hitchins' Lotus 78 as the drizzle intensified before Hitchins was black flagged because his rear wing was falling off. From there is was off to the intense heat of Anderstorp where Bob Berridge's RAM was fastest in qualifying and led from flag to flag. He had missed the previous round with an overheating engine but his Cosworth was now back to full fitness and he made the best of it. Hitchins suffered more bad luck, this time with a blown engine while fighting for second place but Michael Schryver's third overall took him into the lead in the championship.

The hot Swedish sun was a distant memory as the cars practised for the Nurburgring round in June. Showers interfere-with both sessions but a quick dash in the dry gave Geoff Farmer's ex-Steffan Bellof Tyrrell 012 pole by a fraction from Bob Berridge and Martin Stretton back on the scene in his Tyrrell.

The closeness of qualifying carried over into the race with Berridge getting the drop on the two Tyrrells. Berridge's RAM couldn't match Stretton's speed but its brakes were better than the older Tyrrell's which was just enough of an advantage to keep Berridge ahead, albeit by only 0.4 secs at the end. It might have been a different story if Stretton hadn't been plagued by a seriously vibrating gearbox which surprisingly held together for the full 12 laps.

Farmer followed his pole position with third place, well ahead of Joaquin Folch who for a change went through a whole race without pitting, to finish ahead of Ermano Ronchi's BT49 and Michael Schryver's ex-Reine Wissell Lotus 72. Schryver's result was enough to keep him in the lead in the championship.

Goodwood Festival of Speed

What is it about Goodwood? What is it that, in just four years, has turned this intimate, relaxed, largely social event into arguably the most important weekend in the classic car year? PETER TOMALIN has his own theories

Louis Vuitton Damier canvas returns.

In 1888, Louis Vuitton created the Damier chequered canvas. More than a century later, this motif retains a timeless elegance and a resolutely contemporary look.
In a tribute to Louis Vuitton's rich history of creative design, the Damier canvas re-emerges in a special series of bags, luggage and accessories.

LOUIS VUITTON

Mayfair, 149 New Bond Street • Knightsbridge, 198/199 Sloane Street • The City, 7 Royal Exchange, Cornhill
Harrods, Ground Floor, Knightsbridge. For more information, please call: 0800-393-304.

John Surtees in the Mercedes W125 Silver Arrow - one of the most powerful racing cars ever built until the turbo era, with 646bhp in the late 1930s

What is it about Goodwood? Well, there's the setting, of course, and the romance of running racing cars through the tree-smudged grounds of an English stately home There's the link with the old Goodwood circuit, inheritor of the Brooklands spirit and symbol of a 'golden age' in motorsport. And the weather's usually pretty good in June. In fact more often than not, Goodwood has, indeed, been glorious.

The cars are an exquisite distillation of 100 years of speed and glamour. Different ones every year, but always thoughtfully chosen - and that takes passion and understanding. For which we must thank Lord March and his small team of advisers, led by historian Doug Nye and auctioneer/racer Robert Brooks.

The drivers are a pretty select bunch, too. Who could resist the chance to steal an autograph or a few words from the likes of Moss and Surtees and Brabham? However young or old you are, you'll find a hero here. But there's something else that sets Goodwood apart. Such weekends, you feel, can't last forever. There's a sense of history in the making; of 'being there'. Last year there was Moss and Jenks, together in the 300SLR for the first time since the Mille Miglia in 1955. There were grown men with tears in their eyes then. This year saw Jose Froilan Gonzalez, the Pampas Bull, now 72, returning to Goodwood for the first time since the early 1950s to drive a V16 BRM just like he did then.

In years to come, people will talk of the moment they saw Gonzalez pull on his yellow cork helmet, battered and apparently riddled with bullet holes (for keeping a cool head, of course) and jam himself into the apple-green BRM. The sight was enough to bring a lump to the throat; the shattering sound of the V16 sent a shiver of excitement across the tarmac.

Later in the paddock, the stocky Argentine, dark eyes gleaming, leant against the car as the crowd gathered. Someone said the right thing, and as the first programme was proferred for an autograph, his face, worn and weathered like the leather seat of

Surtees again, still the only man ever to have won world championships on four wheels and two, this time preparing to demonstrate his MV Agusta

an old racing car, cracked into a smile. It was no use fighting it. Even the Pampas Bull had to give in to the Goodwood effect.

It's a series of magic moments woven into an unforgettable whole. Even the cynical are won over. And yes, with Sunday so crowded that they may limiting ticket sales, maybe Goodwood is becoming a victim of its own success; but could it be any other way? It has its share of poseurs, too; but at its core the throng is real enthusiast, and the enthusiasm infects young and old alike.

Youngsters turn up to see Eddie Irvine in a Grand Prix Ferrari and are given the show of their lives. But they're also swept away by the sight, sound and smell of ancient chain-driven monsters. Old-car types go to see Gonzalez and Moss and are dazzled by the ferocious speed and noise of a modern Formula 1 car.

There are bikes, too; this year John Surtees assembled a mouthwatering collection of MV Agustas, and riders to match, including Phil Read and Sammy Miller. And aeroplanes; on Saturday, Spitfires, on Sunday an RAF Harrier's incredible aerial ballet. Goodwood burns a series of images into the memory, and everyone comes away with a different set. These are mine.

Saturday morning practice runs, and a 1904 11.2-litre Peerless Green Dragon gets proceedings under way. Then comes the growling 16-cylinder Bugatti Type 45, and the Alfa 8C-35, crackling and popping, igniting the atmosphere and bringing the hill to life, as the sun starts to chase the chill from the air.

Surtees approaches the start in the 646bhp Mercedes W125, waves of revs crashing through the trees, then clouds of tyre-smoke as he launches it off the line, whipping at the wheel to keep the Silver Arrow straight. Standing at the start, you can follow its progress all the way up the hill, a brutal multi-cylinder blare that rises and falls with every gearchange.

What a contrast is next, the Panhard et Levassor, 100 years old and standing twice the height of any other car here. The driver gets the signal, and . . . it's off. Or is it? Yes, wreathed in steam and smoke, with whirrings and meshings as the driver stirs the box. In the Paris-Marseilles-Paris race of 1896, it completed 1080 miles in a numbing 67 hours 42 minutes and 58 seconds.

Eventually it clears the hill, and we're treated to the savagery of a V16 BRM, sounding like a whole grid of cars. Then comes Moss in the Mercedes W196, rolling back the years in white, open-face helmet and powder-blue overalls. And on it goes: the deep, guttural note of the Formula 1 Scarab, a plume of smoke from the torpedo-tail of the Miller Golden Submarine, built in 1917 for cigar-chewing American showman racer Barney Oldfield and surely the most extraordinary looking car of the weekend; Gary Pearson balancing the JCB D-type on the throttle - one of the quickest cars, and drivers, in historic racing today.

Thrust SSC, Richard Noble's twin jet Land Speed Record car has arrived to take pride of place in front of the House. Now that would make an interesting entry for the hillclimb. It's ringed by the most fantastic array of Jaguars, including no fewer than six long-nose D-types and the unique V12-engined XJ13, never raced, but arguably the most beautiful of all Jaguars.

At the bottom of the paddock, another batch of cars is waiting to leave the assembly area. Spectators are pressed to the

On track and in paddock, crowds can get closer to the cars at Goodwood than ever they would at a modern event - to ogle every era of Ferrari, or maybe to eavesdrop on Moss and Bell in their two generations of Porsche

World champions of two eras at Goodwood. the 'Pampas Bull', Froilan Gonzalez, was reunited with V16 BRM, and Phil Hill with F1 Ferrari. A nice contrast in headgear, too

fence, inches from the action, breathing lungfuls of fumes, fingers jammed into ears, grinning madly. The paddock is an essential part of the Goodwood experience, with free access to cars and drivers alike. By late morning it's swarming and everywhere you look there's something special. I almost trip over the ground-hugging snout of a Ford F3L. This rare and beautiful late-1960s GT car is seldom seen; today at Goodwood there are three of them.

Hard-charging Don Orosco has had an 'off' in the Scarab sports car. They're beating out its battered nose with hammers. It will be back in action before the afternoon is out. Jack Brabham, in shades, is signing autographs by the Repco Brabham, besieged by fans. A marshall waits to get his overalls signed by ebullient Aussie Frank Gardner. A whistle warns that there's a car coming through, and as the crowd parts there is the sight of a Gulf GT40 and a Gulf Porsche 917 coming down the paddock lane.

There's Nick Mason climbing out of an early 1970s Ferrari 512 Spider. And one of the cars it was built to beat, a Porsche 917, is shaping up for a head-on collision with another Porsche, the outrageous 935/78 - Moby Dick - a sort of a cross between a 911 and a nightmare. Derek Bell, fresh from the previous weekend's Le Mans, seems to be driving it the wrong way through the paddock. As the world's most expensive traffic jam begins to form, Derek leaps out and leaves the car to a Porsche mechanic.

Cosworth DFV-powered Ford F3L made a rare appearance - in fact three of them were here. Designed by Len Bailey, it was a successor to the GT40

Eddie Irvine didn't go for the hill record but delighted the crowds with a spectacular exhibition of modern Ferrari F1 power, and tyre smoke

Bell had demonstrated the twin-turbocharged monster the previous weekend at Le Mans, where it ran unsuccessfully in 1978 (not helped by needing refuelling every 30 minutes). What's it like, then? 'Oh, it's wild. 850bhp is rather a lot, isn't it?', he chuckles. 'Especially on tyres that were built in 1949. . .'

Does it understeer? 'Just a tad. You turn the wheel, press the accelerator and it goes straight on. Then another 500bhp comes in and wheee: all of a sudden you're doing tank-slappers all the way up the straight'. What time did he do? 'I don't even know if I'm being timed. It doesn't really matter anyway . . .'

Klaus Bischof, Bell's former race engineer, now manager of the Porsche Museum, is Moby Dick's minder for the weekend. He's typical of the unsung heroes of the Festival and is all smiles. 'It's just the best historic event in Europe', he says. 'It's the place and the people - they're so interested, so knowledgable, but they don't touch the cars, and there's no stress, no pressure'.

Sunday; the crowds are back, and this time they've brought their mates with them. Unlike pre-war Brooklands, there's plenty of crowding, but it's still the right crowd. Everyone remains remarkably good-humoured; I spend some time at the start line again. Surtees puts on a display of pyrotechnics just getting to the start line in the W125, spitting flames through a gale of wheel-spin. In one batch there's Gonzalez in the BRM, Moss in the

Mercedes and Brabham in the Cooper. A real slice of history.

In the afternoon the serious business begins. Only about half the cars are being timed up the 1.16-mile course, but don't let anyone kid you that the drivers aren't trying. Nick Mason in a Bugatti Type 35B (66.86secs), Robert Brooks in a Maserati 8CM (62.67) and Paul Grist, just pipped in his Alfa 8C-35 (63.05), set the pace in the pre-war cars, while Rick Hall takes it up with Tom Wheatcroft's 1954 Mk II BRM (in a dramatic 61.94).

In the paddock I find Simon Draper, a regular front-runner in historic racing, with his pretty Lancia B20 Corsa. He's brought his Aston Martin Project 214, too. The Lancia is struggling against the Ferraris and Masers in the 1950s Mille Miglia class, but the 1960s GT class looks close, with the three Aston 'Project' cars taking on the GTOs and Lightweight E-types. And so it proves, with Gary Pearson scorching up the hill in Brandon Wang's GTO in just 58.58 seconds, and Draper second in 59.34.

Simon doesn't pretend they're not trying, but he makes the point that the festival has changed over the years. 'In the early years it was the same bunch of enthusiasts who go historic racing in Britain, so naturally that was pretty competitive. But it's grown. Now it's not just the British historic car scene; it's a truly international event. And they are choosing cars more for the spectacle now, which is fair enough. Every year they're refining it, and

Alfa Romeo part of paddock brought together sports and GP cars from an era when Ferrari was team boss

The enthusiasm never fades. Stirling Moss rolled back the years in both F2 Porsche and F1 Mercedes W196, quick as ever

Two different decades of all-American motor racing muscle were represented by 1950s Cunningham and 1960s Ford Galaxie. Ford was Jack Sears' championship winner. The Cunningham was built mainly for Le Mans

this seems to be the best organised yet. It's different every year, but what I like, what doesn't change, is the atmosphere'.

Stirling Moss is one star who keeps coming back. 'It's such a wonderful occasion', he says. 'And what always amazes me is that all these people behave so well. You don't see lager louts or people abusing the cars. These are real fans'.

This year, as well as the W196, he's driving an F2 Porsche 787. 'I drove one like it in Rob Walker blue in 1960', he says. 'Very nice, six-speed gearbox, and quite a pushy engine. They've told me to keep the revs to seven here, though obviously if you were racing you'd use a lot more. The engine was strong, and although the car is quite heavy compared with the Coopers and so on, you could make up for it because you could drive it really hard. Like all Porsches it's immensely strong and reliable. You didn't find wheels coming off . . . I have some good memories of the car, including racing at Goodwood'.

Away from the racing cars, there are acres of trade stands, the Brooks auction, the art gallery, and the Cartier 'Style et Luxe' concours - sublime coachbuilt gems, ranged on the lawn to the left of the House, jazz from the bandstand. The judges include architect Sir Norman Foster and style ambassador Sir Terence Conran. I don't envy them the task. I simply couldn't choose between the 1932 Bugatti T50T 'profilée', the 1938 Voisin C28 drophead, and the delicious 1937 Delahaye 135M.

Back in the paddock are the weird and wonderful. Within a few yards are the Golden Submarine, the Bugatti 'Tank', and most outlandish of all, the Voisin Laboratoire - whose driver is wearing a 1920s spacesuit and Buck Rogers-style winged helmet.

The variety of cars is one of the things that makes this event so appealing. Dwarfing the sports cars is the vast 7-litre Ford Galaxie which Jack Sears drove to the British Saloon Car Championship in 1963, and sitting inside is Gentleman Jack himself. It's an unlikely looking car for a hillclimb, I suggest.

'Well, nobody thought it would handle, or stop, in the 1960s either', he smiles. 'When the John Willment racing team brought it to Britain, it was a bit of an unknown quantity. But the first time I drove it, I knew it was something special. It was built for NASCAR, of course, by Holman and Moody; it had 450bhp, four shock absorbers at the front, lots of glassfibre panels to save weight, and it did 185mph at Daytona.

'In Britain, it was up against the 3.8-litre Jaguars. Even when it beat them at Silverstone, everyone said it would lose out on smaller, tighter circuits. But it didn't. It was just as quick as the Jaguars through corners, and on the straights it left them for dead. With the exception of the six-hour race at Brands, where I was driving a Cortina GT, the Jaguars didn't win another race.

This particular Galaxie went to South Africa in 1965, where it won another championship, then went into storage. Jack finally managed to buy it back in 1989, and now fully restored it's a fantastic sight. 'It's a bit wide, I suppose, but it still handles. Its Achilles heel is the clutch; you have to trickle it off the line, but then you can give it a bootful'. And of course, he does.

For me, it's another of the highlights of the Festival, but there are so many: Buck Boudeman's stunning Blue Crown Special, the last front-engined car to win Indianapolis, in 1949; the three Ford MkIIs which finished first, second and third at Le

Mans in 1966 and the perfect example of this year's 'Dream Teams' theme; Michelle Mouton blasting up the hill in 51 seconds in the Audi Quattro to be fastest lady driver of the day.

Charles March has had a typically dizzying weekend, playing the perfect host, passengering on a 160mph racing sidecar combination, and driving the jewel-like Porsche 908/3 Spyder up the hill each day. Designed for the narrow, twisting roads of the Targa Florio (which it won in 1970), it's a natural for Goodwood. 'I think I've fallen on my feet', he laughs. 'Only problem is, it should be about the quickest car here. But I'm not being timed. I don't mind looking a bit stupid going slowly, but I don't want to look very stupid sticking it into one of the bails!'

And how does this year's Festival compare with previous years? 'For me, this is the best one yet, by a mile. I mean, to have Thrust here, and McLaren, and Ferrari . . .'

Ah yes, the F1 Ferrari. When Eddie Irvine approaches the line for his first Sunday run, I make it to trackside, halfway up the hill, just in time to hear his tyre- spinning start over the PA. A few seconds later, the Ferrari comes into view, and Fast Eddie appears to have broken it, as the brilliant red projectile comes to a halt just feet away. But then all hell breaks loose. There is a scream from the engine, the tyres light up, and the car charges madly forward, slewing sideways and calling on all Eddie's skill to keep it on the narrow track. Then it's gone, and the crowd cheers. I feel like I've been struck by lightning, and I look at the track. Two thick black lines of rubber, a hundred yards long.

If he'd been trying for a fast time rather than putting on a show, who knows? But he leaves that to Jonathan Palmer, the

master of the hill, who duly obliges with a new record in the Cosworth-powered Williams FW07B. 45 seconds dead, 1.6 seconds inside his old mark. Sensational stuff on a sensational day.

The single most impressive figure of the weekend is the attendance: some 86,000 people, more than any other historic car event. Yet despite its international flavour, it is still somehow very English. Where else can you imagine the PA announcing to the paddock, 'Mr Gonzalez will not be running the V16 BRM until later today, since he is at present enjoying breakfast in bed'?

I for one hope things like that never change, that it remains a family event, only even more so. If they can keep the real enthusiasts coming and avoid too much overt commercialism, that will help, too. The Goodwood Festival is the antidote to so much that's wrong with modern motorsport. May it always be so.

Even earlier American era was seen in the lovely Miller Special. W196 engine showed ultimate GP technology of 1950s, with injection and supercharging

March Heir

Goodwood was once one of Britain's finest circuits. After the war it took on much of the atmosphere that Brooklands offered before it. Now Goodwood House has the Festival of Speed and Goodwood circuit has a new future, thanks to the efforts of the enthusiastic Lord March. KEVIN BRAZENDALE heard the happy news

Friday the 13th. Not, perhaps, the day you would choose to meet a man who is nervously waiting to hear a planning decision that could make or break two and half years of hard work. Luckily I didn't know that the call was coming. Luckier still, when the phone rang it was good news. The vote of the local authority Development Control Committee charged with considering the plans to resume racing at Goodwood circuit was almost unanimous. With 15 to 2 in favour, acceptance was recommended to the full District Council.

It wasn't the end of the battle but it was certainly a major step forward, and Charles Henry Gordon Lennox, Earl of March and Kinrara, owner of Goodwood, was delighted. But then he's had a lot to be delighted about recently, particularly in the overwhelming success of the Goodwood Festival of Speed, and it doesn't take you long on first acquaintance to feel his enormous enthusiasm for the Festival and anything else to do with motor cars and motor racing.

Go from the reception room in Lord March's Goodwood House office to the office itself and from being surrounded by paintings of horses and the Goodwood four-legged race track you move into another century, and a world of motor racing. Posters from the circuit's glory days cover every wall, there's a huge illustration of how the track will be when racing returns; and in a corner is the Scott Gaze Trophy, waiting to be presented once again to the fastest British driver at Goodwood, after a gap of over 30 years.

With Lord March being President of the British Automobile Racing Club and a patron of both the TT Riders Association and the Brooklands Society, motor racing is clearly in the blood, even though it apparently skipped a generation with Lord March's father. But go back to his grandfather, the ninth Duke of Richmond and Gordon, and it is obvious where the inspiration comes from.

As a young man, the Duke left Oxford before he was pushed. He spent so much time at Brooklands that it would, by all accounts, have been a truly academic exercise for him to have turned up for his finals.

Oxford served one purpose though. There he became friends with MG founder Cecil Kimber and when Kimber got MG rolling, Freddie, as he was known, got a drive at Brooklands in 1929. By this time he had already become Lord March, and in 1930 he went on to share the winning supercharged Austin Seven with Sammy Davis in the Brooklands BRDC 500 - probably Austin's greatest racing victory. He then helped to give MG its first major win, at the 1931 Brooklands Double Twelve. His team of three C-type MGs took the team prize while he shared the winning car.

Obviously a talented driver, he was also an excellent organiser, and as his teams' successes showed, he had the gift of motivating people. He moved on to car styling, and his March Special bodies graced chassis from AC to Wolseley. He built models, founded an aircraft company and still found time to be a fine painter and photographer.

Men so talented in so much can be a lot to live up to but in the earlier Lord March's case those talents were combined with great warmth and affection. Pictures can lie but the one of him at Brooklands next to his MG in 1931 apparently doesn't; smiling broadly, he was by all accounts as friendly, open and relaxed as he seems there.

Goodwood in its glorious heyday attracted the best in the world. In the 1953 Goodwood Trophy, Fangio's V16 BRM lines up alongside Moss's Cooper

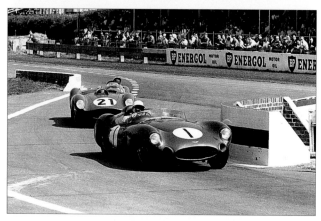

Moss again, in Aston Martin at the 1959 TT, leading through the notoriously solid chicane, shortly before his car was destroyed by fire in the pits

And the essence of Goodwood in the 1950s - the start of the 1954 Easter Monday Formula One race, watched by Lord March himself, with cane, on right

Earlier days for Freddie March, relaxed and smiling by the MG Midget with which he won the 1931 Brooklands Double Twelve

As the present Lord March puts it, 'I was very close to my grandfather and going to the track was the highlight of my year. It was fantastic coming to the house too, as a child. My grandmother was a wonderfully warm person and there were always lots of presents. It was a child's dream, particularly with all the cars'.

The seeds for the circuit, indeed for the Festival, and for so much else, were sown by Lord March's grandfather. In 1935 he organised a competition for members of the Lancia Owners Club, in the grounds of Goodwood House. The programme included a hillclimb, which he won, in his own Lancia. . .

He also gave the go ahead for the Goodwood circuit, but he didn't design it himself. 'We have some draughtsman at the Ministry of Defence to thank for that', explains Lord March, 'and for probably the fastest right hand corner on any British track.

'What's now the circuit was just the perimeter track around the wartime airfield built on Goodwood land. After the war loads of enthusiasts were looking for somewhere to have a race track. They looked all over the place, and as far as Ireland, but it was Tony Gaze who came up with the notion that Goodwood would

make a great circuit. He went to my grandfather and suggested that they take a look at it. Grandfather got in the car, drove around the perimeter road, showed some other people - who all said "marvellous" - and that was that'.

Tony Gaze was a wartime fighter pilot, as was his brother Scott who was killed on a Spitfire sortie from Goodwood. And that explains the shape of the Scott Gaze Trophy. A bronze Spitfire, in flight, dominates a trophy which had already been presented to the likes of Hawthorn, Moss, Parnell and Stewart, before motor racing at Goodwood came to a halt in 1966.

By that time, of course, Lord March was hooked on the sport, despite his very earliest memories of the track being rather mixed. 'I suppose I was about eight or so, and my grandfather took me. We had a little caravan down by the chicane and if I remember rightly it was all rather grim and cold. . . lots of cold sausages and hard boiled eggs', he says, laughing at the memory. 'I can also remember Prince Michael taking me to the track in his new green E-type; and of course I had all the right passes, which helps. I used to meet all the drivers and get their autographs'.

And although Lord March couldn't drive around the circuit as a youngster, there was nothing to stop him hurtling up and down the roads at Goodwood House in anything from a Morgan three-wheeler to a Zip kart. So, inevitably perhaps, 'The idea of having cars whizzing up the hill has always been something I'd thought about but without ever really thinking it was possible. It wasn't until Ian Bax of the BARC asked me one day if I'd ever considered holding an event here that I really did consider it; and there was also always great support from the RAC.

'That was in the October; we just said "right we're doing it" and the first Festival happened the following June. Everyone said we'd maybe get two or three thousand people but even I had no idea we'd get the 25,000 or whatever it was that we did get.

'The Festival of Speed has the advantage of being at an ideal location in the middle of summer but there's more to its success than that. It's different in that you can't just enter. All the cars are selected to fit a theme and we try to get hold of cars that no one ever sees. The theme makes us focus on that, and the last thing we want to see is the same cars trotted out every year. Next

Goodwood 1996-style, on a beautiful summer's day. The House plays host to the Festival of Speed, now one of the biggest events of the season

BRITISH MOTOR

And its all going to change. We're not talking about changing our products; we have always striven to improve and introduce new parts. We use original tools when we can for the best possible fit - and we

HERITAGE IS ALL

will continue to do so. But quality of product is not enough - we are committed too improving our service. Soon you'll see an enhanced network of Heritage Approved Specialists appearing across the world.

ABOUT QUALITY,

Many of the names you'll already know, but they are all specialists in their field, craftsmen and experts who supply our products directly to you. And our criteria for selecting these "Approved Specialists"?

ORIGINALITY

Simply, that they share our commitment to quality, originality and above all else, they share our belief in good service. We feel that these days, that shouldn't be too much to ask.

AND SERVICE…

BRITISH MOTOR HERITAGE

year will be very different again. Better than ever, I hope; and there are some cars we've been trying to get for a couple of years that might actually make it next time. People are fantastically willing but, even so, persuading some of the great museums that they should get their cars out to celebrate some motoring anniversary or other can be very difficult'.

As for the circuit itself, it promises to combine old traditions with modern demands, and serious concessions had to be made to get approval for the resumption of racing.

'We've been through about three years of negotiations with the local authority', says Lord March, 'and it's been a massive trade off. There will be 100 quiet days at the track and it won't be used on any Sundays except the two race weekends. Anyone opposed to it would have to be bonkers not to see that what's on offer is far better than what's there at the moment. Currently the circuit is busy for 280, 290 days a year and there are sprints and tests and so on there. Nevertheless some of the opposition campaigned for there to be no activity there at all. Well, that was never an option.

'We've already got planning permission for the track to be a race track and they can't take that away. The fact that we haven't held a race here for so long is irrelevant'.

As to what form future events at the re-opened circuit will take, Lord March has few doubts. It will revolve around historic racing, naturally. 'We've got two race weekends. I'm keen not to have more as I don't think we can sustain more and the racing has to be the best there is. Really Goodwood is the perfect place. It's still intact and it was so much the place

Charles March, racing driver, at Silverstone with freshly prepared 1958 Lola sports racer. He only wishes he'd started earlier

Perks of the job. Lord March in Gulf Porsche at 1996 Festival. When the race circuit re-opens he intends to be on the front of the grid

ASTON MARTIN LAGONDA LIMITED

MAINTAINING THE TRADITION

Works Service Newport Pagnell
For unparalleled levels of care, knowledge
and traditional craftsmanship.

There is only one Works.
There is only one Works Service.

For further information and advice please contact
Keith Riddington, Andrew McCloskey or David Webb
on our 24 hour direct line - 01908 619264.

Tickford Street, Newport Pagnell, Buckinghamshire, England MK16 9AN
Telephone 01908 610620. Fax 01908 216439

The Festival works hard to attract cars which aren't seen too often. 1996 saw a rare non-GP outing for a works Ferrari, and exuberant Eddie Irvine

to be after the war, just as Brooklands was before it. From 1948 to 1966 it had all the cars that people want to see now. And I hope it won't affect the other historic events, as the historic scene is growing so much. . .'

So, once the circuit itself does re-open for racing, will the Festival move there? 'No', says Lord March emphatically. 'The Festival of Speed will continue to be in June and stay where it is, up at the house. That and the racing are two very different things, and probably appeal to different markets. For one thing, the owners of some of the cars we get here would never allow them on the circuit, certainly not to race on it;

but they can come here and at least give the impression they are going quickly'.

And a time scale? Well, a great deal of work has to be done before Lord March's dream is reality, with some massive sound deadening earth banks being thrown up, buildings refurbished and others built. But there is a tempting target. 'It would be wonderful' he says, 'to get it ready for 1998 - which would be 50 years after it first opened. And we'd get Tony Gaze over from Australia to see it. That would be marvellous but it would be an awful lot of work. . .'

One thing that's for certain is that Lord March will be out there on the track for the occasion. He has started to compete in a 1958 Lola, restored earlier this year. 'I love it, I wish I'd done it a lot earlier. That first grid will be hand picked by me and I'll be on the front row! Come to think of it, then I'd be expected to win the bloody race, so maybe I'd be better off being the good host, starting at the back and coming last. . .'

False modesty? No, you get the impression that Lord March has nothing to prove and simply enjoys his racing for the sheer fun of it, 'I should know the track', he agrees. 'I've hacked round it enough over the years. And I'm reasonably good when there's no one else around; but the thing about racing is that you've suddenly got 20 other cars all round you. It makes it a bit tougher. Still that first race will be a bit of a moment. Mustn't get over excited though. . .'

With luck we will only have a couple of years to wait before the promise gets put to the test and the spirit of Goodwood rises again. After all, it's all in the family.

L'AGE D'OR, MONTLHERY 22-23 June

Montlhery is a bit like Brooklands, a legend, much loved but much abused. Like Brooklands, it's an old, banked circuit which no one has the will or the money properly to repair. But while the sadly truncated Brooklands track lies silent, racing still goes on at the Paris circuit, and principally in L'Age d'Or, literally the Golden Age meeting.

Even this won't, perhaps, run for much longer; but while it is still held, it offers an unrivalled opportunity to see racing at one of the world's oldest circuits. And contrary to popular image, Montlhery isn't simply a flat-out banking; there are three chicanes, the most memorable of them being the one where the cars pour down from the banking before the pits, and those are complemented by a couple of first gear hairpins.

As at the Coys Silverstone Festival you'll see many races over the weekend and a superb selection of cars. 'Golden Age' is interpreted generously, from the 1920s through to the 1960s, and large fields of classic saloons might see Mustangs and Falcons squabbling with Alfa Giulias and GTV, Minis and Anglias.

ERAs, Cooper Bristols and Maserati 250Fs appear together too, and Bugatti 35s battle it out with Rileys and MGs. Again as at Silverstone some of the racing can be intense; Jason Wright's Cooper-Bristol was a mere half a second behind Philip Walker's winning Lotus 16, for example, in race four.

It does help, however, if you have cars built like lorries and Ettore Bugatti once described Bentleys as the fastest in the world. This year, there were 12 of them at L'Age d'Or, entered by the Benjafields Racing Club whose members were intent on recreating the marque's 1927 Montlhery win, this time in the Prewar Sports Racing event. They were up against Astons, MGs and various Delahayes, Bugattis and Amilcars. But in the end, while Stanley Mann did his best for Bentley, he couldn't match the pace of Marc Hevier's Alvis and Jean-Louis Duret's Bugatti Type 35. It was a disappointment, but who knows: maybe next year. . .

The old track may not survive much longer but while it's there drivers make the most of it, their cars streaming down off the Montlhery banking here, through one of the chicanes

The three tight chicanes are almost as much a feature of the circuit as the banking and put a strain on upright saloons like this Volvo

This Delage straight-eight could have been racing on the Montlhery banking when the track was in its prime

Removing the front wing put the Phillips and Moss Cortina, right, out of the running in an Ypres Historic won by local driver Robert Droogmans in a Porsche 911. He finished ahead of Neil Calvert's Cortina in second place. The Whitney A110, below, couldn't equal the fine performance of the other Alpine driven by Ricard Tyzack, which finished seventh

5-12 JULY
Rallye des Alpes

A week of freak weather preceded this year's Rallye des Alpes, but still the competitors came, with 73 cars in all, to take on the challenge issued by organiser Roland Gassman to tackle some of the toughest roads in the Swiss, French and Italian Alps. And starting in Geneva on Friday evening they also had to brave some of the worst summer weather for decades. Incessant rain poured from a thunderous sky, with lightning thrown in.

The drivers stood around in damp huddles under their umbrellas, waiting for the start, unable to do the usual last minute fettling for fear of drowning their machines; and the navigators fretted over their own problems while waiting for their instructions to be given, just before the off. It didn't help that the first section was a night one, through the French Jura Mountains north of Geneva. With the route book containing the bare minimum of information, some crews broke the first rule of rally navigation: don't follow anyone. Small packs of cars got lost and tried to turn around on roads no wider than they were. All the crews took penalties on this stage; even the best, Lacomblez in a DKW Auto Union took 684, and half got maximum penalties. All were glad to reach the finish in the early hours.

The weather was no better the next day, into the Haute Savoie, the route dipping and diving through the trees, up through the clouds into the sunlight and back into the murk. Navigation again was extremely tough. Following the Rhone valley up to Ulrichen the rally turned east towards the Nufenen pass with a welcome break in the weather. The steep climb and repetitive hairpins found large gaps in some cars' gear ratios and crews

Looking more like a scene from the Monte Carlo Challenge this is the Alps in July with the Mustang's lights blazing to pierce the murk, right. Momentarily blinded by the photographer's flash the MG TF corners hard

Once the cars were well into the mountains, left, navigation became simpler; when there is only one road, that's the one you follow. The Verbeecxs' big Healey, right, splashes through the rain which blighted the first two days

crept past the buildings at the top of the pass, at 2478 metres high, where winter persists long after it's summer in the valley.

Over the pass the rally followed the course of the Ticino river, into Italian-speaking Switzerland with the sun finally bursting through to illuminate the mountain villages. The lower slung cars bumped and grounded on the cobbled streets of one, with the locals out in force looking on. When the Aston Martin of Hofer and Pouponnet pulled over, cakes and drinks appeared, and an impromptu party began. The locals were invited to try the car out for size and the bolder ones took it in turns to climb in, grip the wheel and pump the pedals.

From Locarno it was on to Domodossaia in Italy via a single track road precariously clinging to the side of the mountain like the single railway line that amazingly managed to follow the same route. Road and railway sinuously intertwined as the railway occasionally disappeared into a tunnel below the road, only to reappear miraculously above it. Snaking around the hills behind Lake Maggiore, the rally returned to the Lake before cutting across to the Aosta valley and up to the Grand St Bernard pass.

When the pass was tackled on the Saturday morning it was engulfed in an unseasonal blizzard. Slipping and sliding to the top was the easy part but the descent would be even more treacherous in the driving snow. Like a huge rollercoaster the cars rushed down the ominously named Mont Mort, through the Aosta valley and up the snow-enveloped Petit St Bernard.

Passing over the Cornet de Roseland the rally passed roads covered in paint-sprayed graffiti. The Tour de France cycle race had passed this way just a few days earlier, famously sharing the same appalling weather, and the paint-sprayed messages are the traditional way for fans to encourage their favourite teams. As the rally approached the beautiful Spa towns of Aix les Bains over the mountains, the weather cleared to reveal alpine scenery at its finest - but any crews hoping for respite were in for a shock as the rally kept up its pace right to the end. The Porsche 911s of van Soom and Glaas tried hard but they couldn't match the consistency shown by Lacomblez's Auto Union and there was now little scope for catching up. With the weather no longer a significant factor, the top teams just had to keep their heads and not get lost to keep their positions and reach the Marseilles finish.

But if the finish sounds easy the rally in its entirety quite definitely wasn't, with 3061km to cover up and down over mountains, hard on the brakes or the throttle most of the time and with almost continuous cornering to contend with. It was enough to break the best of cars and dishearten the strongest of crews. For most, it did neither, but it did lift them from the realms of everyday existence to the very heights of historic rallying.

This Swiss MG crew improvised their own design of plastic side screens in a bid to prevent their cockpit from becoming totally flooded

A Maserati
3500 *down from
the mountains.
Along the roads
in the valleys
between the
countless ascents
the crews' navi-
gational skills
were severely
put to the test*

AMOC BRANDS HATCH 6-7 *July*

The Aston Martin Nimrod may have enjoyed only a brief and not very bright racing career in its heyday, and more recently it only managed a couple of laps in the June St John Horsfall meeting, but it made up for that - twice over - at Brands Hatch.

First John Dennehy took it to the flag in the postwar Aston Martin race, despite starting with a 20-second penalty and despite having seen Ronnie Farmer in the lead for the first five laps in his DB4, until Farmer suffered an unusual failure. As Dennehy clawed back the seconds, the strain of leading proved too much for, of all things, Farmer's gearlever - which snapped off in his hand. So Farmer didn't even rescue second place, and behind the Nimrod in the end came the rather less advanced DB4 of Pete Foster, carrying on where he left off from his similarly fine performance in the last race at Silverstone in the St John Horsfall meeting the previous month.

July's Brands Hatch event may lack the scope of that meeting but it makes up for it with the greater visual appeal of the Kent circuit and, like the St John Horsfall attracts far more than just Aston Martins. Indeed it wasn't until the fifth race of the two-day programme that there was a race exclusively for Astons. The club has to be congratulated for putting on a varied display which included an International Spridget race, won by Rae Davis's Midget, which also won the MG v Austin Healey event.

Pete Foster improved on his second place in the postwar Astons race with a good win in the Goldsmith and Young Thoroughbred Sports Car race. His DB4 finished ahead of the sister car of familiar rival Ed Sharpe, although earlier on, Joe Ward had seemed set to beat both of them before being forced to slow.

Winning then became an even more familar feeling for Foster as, partnered by Ian Moss, he won the first Endurance race on the Saturday - although despite his best efforts he could not repeat the feat on Sunday. In that second race the Ronnie Farmer/ Geoff Harris partnership finished ahead of Ashdown and Parnell's Lotus Elan, and the Chevrolet Camaro of Boley Pritchard, but with an Aston winning each leg, the team prize, not suprisingly, went to Foster/Moss and Farmer/Harris.

John Dennehy's second win with the Nimrod came in the ERF Intermarque race, which Malcolm Hamilton's Jaguar V12 E-type had led until half distance. Dennehy overhauled him, however, and went on to win (albeit by just a two-second margin) with Richard Chamberlain's Porsche 911 RSR back in third place and ahead of Ronnie Farmer in fourth.

MGs and Austin Healeys had also been invited into the Aston Martin fold. Here, Graham Ball's DB4 cuts a path through a clutch of MGs including Brian Lambert's B and Graeme Willard's earlier, 1964 B (78)

Ronnie Farmer thought he was having a good day, leading for five laps of the postwar Aston race but then the DB4 gearlever snapped off in his hand

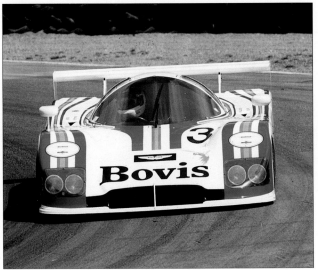

The Aston Martin Nimrod had managed only two laps at the Silverstone meeting but made up for that with a pair of wins at Brands Hatch

There was scope for other heavy metal apart from the Astons at Brands, such as Trevor Pritchard's battle scarred 1968 Chevrolet Camaro

FERRARI NURBURGRING *19-21 July*

The combination of Greenpeace and the Brent Spa was very bad news indeed for Shell's image in Germany and for the past year Shell has been making enormous efforts to repair the damage.

Backing Schumacher was an obvious move, and that meant reviving the old alliance with Ferrari that dated back to the first Formula One World Championship season; with the F1 cars once again bearing Shell logos the company decided it might as well go the whole hog and the Shell/Ferrari alliance can now be seen in things like the Ferrari races at the Nurburgring, run under the banner of the Shell Historical Challenge.

The lure of the Nurburgring, albeit the current F1 circuit rather than the old Nordschleife, was quite enough to draw a breathtaking array of Ferraris, with 250s being the most prominent with 12 in all, including two 250 GTOs, a 250 MM, 250 LM and a 250 Testa Rossa, accompanied by a 500 TR. In age they ran the whole gamut from Sally Mason-Styrron's 1950 166 MM to Walo Schibler's 1970 512 M.

There were cars even older than the Mason-Styrron 166, too, as some particularly interesting Alfas were invited into the fold, so Paul Grist's 8C 35 was there along with Klaus Werner's familiar Monza, Robert Fink's P3, Thomas Feierabend's Monza and the 8C from the eclectic stable of Karl Bloechle. Nobody, of course, pretends any of these cars is competing on anything like equal terms and it hardly matters.

Inevitably Walo Schibler's 512 M won both races, averaging 132kph in the first race and 130kph in the hard-fought second round; there's consistency. The first race included the notable scalp of Gary Pearson, driving a 1965 250 LM, who finished second some 25 seconds adrift. On the second day Pearson dropped back to third, behind the intense battle for the lead between Tommy Setrab Brorsson's 1966 206 S and the Schibler 512 M which Schibler won by a mere 0.872 seconds.

Bart Rosman's was one of six 250 GTs and came home a very respectable seventh in race one, and in ninth the following day

Corrado Cupellini's 206 SP, right, was consistency itself, finishing fourth in both races. An expensive pack of cars, below, with Ernst Schuster's 500 TR ahead of the yellow sister car of David Cottingham

Do you think they know something you don't?

Buyers

- 80 carefully selected cars to choose from.

- The best sale rate in the U.K.
  - on average 78% this year
  (We try not to waste your time with unrealistic reserves).

- Only 5% Buyers Premium (minimum £100).

- Vintage, Veteran, Thoroughbred, Classic and Collectors cars - something for everybody.

- The special H & H Service package - and a wonderful atmosphere.

- Venue - Grade II listed building (as pictured).

Sellers

- Where else can you advertise your car for only £75 and have over 2000 people see the car?

- And if it sells (and it very probably will) only 5% commission (minimum £100).

- We send you your money in 8 working days.

- A very knowledgeable and approachable team.

- Excellent prices including many records established.

- Our sales take place at the elegant Pavilion Gardens in Buxton (as pictured), Derbyshire - the heart of England and easy to get to.

- Many international and private buyers.

H&H

CLASSIC AUCTIONS

**ENTRIES ARE NOW INVITED FOR OUR FUTURE SALES.
SPACES ARE LIMITED, SO TO AVOID DISAPPOINTMENT CALL TODAY.**

For entry forms, catalogues or simply more information on our sale dates please
call either Mark Hamilton or Simon Hope on 0161 747 0561, or fax us on 0161 747 2839
and join the growing number of enthusiasts enjoying the H & H difference.

Augie Pabst, left, was out in a Scarab and finished eighth in the car he raced back in the 1960s. David Hobbs drove Jim Bartel's Simoniz Lola T-163, right, at undiminished speed

19-21 JULY

Chicago Historics

The West Coast has the Monterey Historics at Laguna Seca: the rest of America has the annual Chicago Historic Races at Elkhart Lake. It's a meeting that can lay claim to having the best American racing on the best track in America, if not the best cars.

But then that depends on your perspective. If you really love cars built after 1960 then the Chicago Historics will appeal to you far more than Monterey. This year for example, there was a thirtieth anniversary celebration of Can-Am racing, and 73 of these beasts appeared, with everything from the Genies and Scarabs that ran in the USSRC road-racing series right up to the Shadow DN4 that raced in the final series proper in 1974. Grids are huge for every race because the four-mile track - probably the second best in the world after Spa - can accommodate more than eighty cars. There were no fewer than 54 pre-1973 single seaters, for instance, and the large capacity GT grid for cars built between 1962 and 1974 drew 58 Porsches, Cobras, GT350s, Corvettes and Ferraris. In total 478 cars started in eight races.

The whole long weekend - it stretches over four days - is incredibly relaxing. Vintage racing in America is basically an excuse to have a party and there's more scope for partying in four days than two. Actual racing is limited, being confined to the Sunday, but there's a huge amount of track time available for anyone who wants it - with timed practice on Thursday, Friday and Saturday morning plus a so-called Qualifying race on Saturday afternoon in which positions are irrelevant but from which times count towards the grid for Sunday's race.

The highlight was obviously the Can-Am reunion. Adding spice to the proceedings was the visit by a posse of front runners from the European SuperSports series, led by Charlie Agg in his McLaren M8F. Chris Chiles (March 717), Peter Hannen (M8F) Richard Eyre (M8F) and Jost Kalisch (BRM P154) also appeared, with a number of Lola T70s and Chevrons for support. In the end the best American car/driver combinations were very evenly matched with the best of the Europeans, proving a good driver is a good driver wherever he comes from. But the Americans were amazed by just how quickly their European visitors came to terms with the track. At the end of practice it was an all-American front row, with current IMSA BMW professional driver Bill Auberlen

Can-Am legend George Follmer, right, was at Elkhart Lake. The winner of the 1972 series in Penske's Porsche 917/10, he was driving a McLaren M8F here. It was black, of course, just like his famous UOP cars were

The Chicago Historics catered for more than just the Can-Am monsters. There were no fewer than 54 cars in the pre-1973 open-wheel racers' ranks, right

on pole in a McLaren M20 alongside veteran Can-Am ace George Follmer in an M8F. Also good to see were other ex-Can-Am front runners David Hobbs in Jim Bartel's Simoniz Lola T-163 and Tony Dean in a Porsche 908. Come the race, Auberlen led from flag to flag, pressured all the way by Agg with Chiles third. Hannen set fastest lap at 113mph but lost track position after getting in a tangle with Kalisch. Follmer's car broke early on and of the other quick Americans only Craig Bennet driving Juan Gonzalez's Lola T-222 ran in the top six, finishing fifth. His brother Kirt had the turbocharged 1972 Shadow Mark III 'anti-Porsche' up in the top six until a front brake shaft broke - fortunately not at the end of the straight, where he was timed at 211mph, the fastest of the weekend.

Away from the top 15 cars, though, this was really only a high speed parade, albeit one that featured many great cars that simply wouldn't venture out into a SuperSports event. Two Porsche 908s, a Ferrari 612P, a Ferrari 512M and a Porsche 917PA were the most exotic cars on show but the Honker, Lola T70 MkIs, McKees and Genies were equally enjoyable.

Therein lies one of the dichotomies of American historic racing: the quality of cars is superb but the quality of driving and racing beyond the front third of the grid is pretty woeful. To give an example, anyone who was five or six seconds off the pace at Spa in a Formula Junior Lotus would be regarded as hopeless; yet there were guys out at Elkhart more than twenty seconds slower than similar cars. This makes the racing potentially more dangerous because on this track a badly driven car which has lots of power is more likely to get in the way of a well-driven smaller-engined car. Drivers in Europe tend to be more experienced, having graduated from other forms of racing or having returned to racing after building up their businesses or careers while in America many of the drivers start in historics late in life.

Neverthless there was some impressive driving on view. It was great to see Augie Pabst and his son Augie Pabst III out in the pre-1965 sports car event, both in Scarabs. Pabst Jr in the unique

Some of the races are rather unequal contests; there are few Cobras and Austin Healeys that can match the speed of the well known JLP Racing Porsche 935, right

Not surprisingly it was a McLaren which dominated the Can-Am reunion, topping 200mph through the Elkhart Lake speed trap

mid-engined car finished four seconds behind the winning LaBoa MlII and Augie finished eighth in the Maister Brauser-liveried front-engined 1958 car that he had raced in the 1960s. This race produced a real rag-tag of cars with Brabham BT-8s and McLaren M1s up against Ferrari Testa Rossas and Mercedes 300SLs.

There was a similarly bizarre mixture in the Group 5 race which matched single seaters with sports racing cars and GTs from 1967 onwards. So while Bobby Brown won as he pleased in his 1974 Formula 5000 Lola T-332 single seater he was followed by a Chevron B19 sports car. Look down the entry list and you would see Porsche RSRs lined up against Formula Atlantic Ralts and Marches, a Cosworth-engined Gulf Mirage Group 6 car against a Porsche 910, a couple of Ford GT40s and even a 1995-vintage Porsche 911 Supercup car. How the spectators make out what is going on, I've no idea. Even in the race for GTs between 1962 and 1975, it was odd to see a beautifully driven Ferrari 250GT SWB mixing it with a Porsche RSR and a Corvette. Tom Benjamin in his 1964 Cobra got my vote for one of the drives of the day, finishing fourth behind a 1973 Porsche RSR, 1970 Trans-Am Mustang 302 and 1966 Corvette roadster.

Contrary to popular opinion American historic racing isn't just about incredibly wealthy collectors. In the Group 2 event you see hordes of 356 Porsches and Austin Healey Sprites while Group 8 is composed almost entirely of relatively low-rent metal - albeit very shiny and well prepared. Jennifer Bretzel won this year in a 1973 Porsche RS from Mark Burgard's 1964 Lotus Elan

but further down the field there were Alfa GTVs and Spiders, Datsun 240Zs, Saab Sonnets and even a Volvo P1800. In many ways this was the best balanced race group.

Exhibition classes at American vintage meetings cater usually for more modern cars that have no place to race, for people who have cars they don't want to run in the heat of battle and for people who want to get out on the track but lack the confidence or the will to race. You're only allowed to pass into the corners if another driver beckons you through, otherwise overtaking is all done on the straights. At the Chicago Historics the exhibition class was still posted as a race despite such rules and Dave Nicholas, a really hard charger of a driver in his 1981 March 817 Can-Am car, was first across the line.

One popular feature at most American vintage race meetings, and here included, is an hour-long endurance event. Basically anyone, whether they own a Mini Cooper or a Porsche 962, can take part and there's a mandatory five-minute pit stop where you can refuel, change drivers or do both. No fewer than 78 cars took part in this, with everything from a Frogeye Sprite to an IMSA Ford Mustang. Briton John Burton, there with the SuperSports contingent, won in his Chevron B26.

All in all the Chicago Historic is a terrific meeting, even though the race groups can be confusing to the ordinary spectator. The sheer breadth of machinery on show is wonderful and there's plenty of evidence that the pick of American old-car drivers try equally as hard as anyone else in the world.

Huge V8s suck a lot of air. In true American historic racer tradition, these inlet trumpets, top, are polished to perfection. This historic racing is an expensive business; it helps to have the right base, above

HSCC CROIX EN TERNOIS *27-28 July*

The French weekend organised by the Historic Sports Car Club in late July was a resounding success. A huge number of cars made the short hop across the channel and the Croix en Ternois circuit saw twenty races over the two days.

Race one, for Historic Road Sports and Thoroughbred Sports Cars, saw Joe Ward's TVR Griffith just get the edge on the Tuscan of Howard Brearley with Roger Arveschongh's Griffith back in third. It was pretty well the same mixture when those cars were out again in round ten, the only difference being that the third place Griffith dropped back to tenth. That wasn't the only event enjoyed by the TVRs, as John Moon put his 3000M into second place (behind Roger Barton's Lotus 7) in the 1970s Road Sports Championship.

Andrew Marler's Elan headed no fewer than four Marcos GTs in the Classic Sports Car Championship but it was a weekend for open wheelers as well as sports cars, with race two the HSCC Single Seater Challenge, won by John Narcisi's Trojan, 4.8 seconds ahead of John Crowson's Argo JM6 and lapping faster than any other car the whole weekend.

Just a few miles per hour slower were the cars in the Chris Alford Historic FF1600 Championship, won by Paul Sleeman in the Jamun T2 at 68.22mph, faster than Geoff Farmer's winning Brabham BT18B in the first Classic Racing Car Series round. In the second round of that, Farmer gave best to Ian Rowley's Delta.

The two Ralt RT1s of Gerd Holtkamp and Ralf Moog topped the weekend's rounds in the German Open Championship. In contrast to the grids in those races, only six cars turned out for the RJB Mining Championship, with Mike Wilds' Chevron B31/36 heading the thin field ahead of George Douglas's Ginetta G12. Not surprisingly the International Spridget Championship was better supported, with 18 entries, Rae Davis finishing ahead of Ad Flipse, both in Midgets.

The grid for the International Spridget Challenge was packed with 18 entries, and included one Sebring Sprite

Harvey Cooke's E-type chases the TR4 of Chris Conoley during the Historic Road Sports race

Gerdo Schepel locks his Frogeye's brakes on his way to ninth in the Spridget Challenge

THE POWER AND THE GLORY

Motor sports and Lynx have always been closely connected over the past 25 years. Currently the Lynx-prepared Ecurie Ecosse Tojeiro-Jaguar finished a very creditable third in the 1996 BRDC Louis Vuitton Sports Car Championship. Its first full season of racing since 1959!

The experience, engineering knowledge and discipline required to consistently succeed in historic racing is applied to all the company's projects. Our in-house facilities include CAD systems for the manufacture and modification of components, a fully-equipped machine shop, aluminium fabrication and race-bred technicians.

For historic race car preparation, event support, consultancy or the restoration and development of your sports car, please contact us to discuss your individual requirements.

LYNX MOTORS
INTERNATIONAL LIMITED

68 Castleham Road St Leonards on Sea
East Sussex TN38 9NU England
Tel 44 (0)1424 851277 Fax 44 (0)1424 853771
E-MAIL enquiries@lynxmotors.co.uk
URL http://www.lynxmotors.co.uk

Coys Festival

Officially, it's the Coys International Historic Festival presented by Chrysler. To most fans, it's known simply as the Coys Festival. Whatever you call it, it's one of the biggest weekends in the classic car year, and KEVIN BRAZENDALE was there to report on the action

A German and an Englishman, wheel to wheel around Silverstone. Earlier in the year that might have meant the British Grand Prix; now the stakes might be lower but no one could question the effort, enthusiasm, excitement, or the sheer skill on display in a different context.

If the 50,000-odd who turned up to the Coys International Historic Festival in August had seen only the first race, they would have had their money's worth, watching Martin Stretton in the 1936 Lagonda 4.5-litre fighting it out with the German pairing of Klaus Werner and Peter Groh in their ex-Nuvolari Alfa Romeo 8C2300.

No contest surely? The Lagonda belongs to the English perpendicular school of car design, powered by a big simple engine; and didn't a similar Lagonda win Le Mans in 1935 only by dint of still being around at the end?

Here it was up against sheer supercharged straight-eight twin-cam class in the model that dominated Le Mans, from 1931 to 1934. So it should have been easy for the Alfa, but Stretton was inspired, right next to Werner and almost touching as he tried to pass on the outside through Becketts on the first lap before getting through on the inside at Stowe. In his efforts to get back on terms, Werner ran well wide on to the dirt at Luffield. By this stage even the uninitiated in the crowd realised this was a real race – as would Mark Gillies as the Lagonda dived in front of his Riley, showering him with dust from the side of the track. Stretton drove the tall Lagonda like a car half the size, always in perfect control, leaning out of the car, drifting it but but never letting it slide away, in a superb demonstration of car control.

The Coys format means you don't get to play all that long in each race, and the Pre War Sports Car Race is a team effort where a co-driver has to do at least a couple of the eight laps. That saw Martin handing over to wife Amanda, who couldn't match the speed of Peter Groh. As Martin explained, 'Amanda hasn't had much practice in this car but she's getting faster all the time. It'll

Sixties icons in the Coys of Kensington GT Race: the AC Cobra of Bryant and Shepherd is chased by a Shelby Mustang

The beauty of Coys is the variety of machinery: everything from pre-war Alfas, left, to the 1960s F1 BRM, above

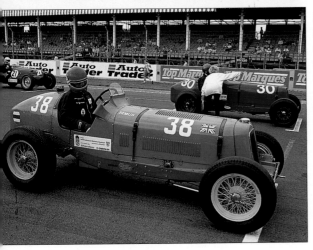

Left, the famous ERA 'Remus' went well in the hands of Ludovic Lindsay - second in Sunday's pre-52 GP Car Race

be closer tomorrow.' That's another feature of the festival. Most of the races were two-stage affairs, held over the Saturday and Sunday. In eight or ten laps there's less chance of over stressing the cars, and a chance to fix them for the next race if something does go wrong on day one.

The victorious Germans were naturally happy, and very complimentary. 'This is the best race meeting for old cars in the whole of Europe,' was Peter Groh's very first comment, echoed by his team mate, Werner: 'I like the new circuit. It's more challenging, harder to learn and harder on brakes.' That will sound odd to someone who's not been to Silverstone for a while and can remember classic cars looking out of their element on the wide expanses of the ultra fast Grand Prix circuit. There are more corners these days, even for the modern Formula One cars, but for the Festival the track had been modified since the British Grand Prix, with another new corner at Vale, while these cars would be using the old Abbey Curve, and Stowe had also been improved. The drivers loved it and from Abbey through Bridge and into the complex of tighter corners at Priory, Brooklands and Luffield towards the end of the circuit, cars were passing and repassing on every lap. The grandstands along the Pit Straight were virtually deserted as the crowds gathered where the action was.

To cater for the huge spread of cars in most races, there are as many classes as are needed – six in all for that first race, for instance, where the field ranged from the quick Lagonda and Alfa to the stately S Type Invictas and miniscule MG C Montlherys. That means that there's racing right through the field, which includes drivers of all ages and experience from 85-year-old Tom Delaney (still competing in the Lea Francis Hyper he drove at Brooklands before the war) to the young Amanda Stretton.

If you've never been to classic racing in Britain you might wonder just how good is the driving at events like Coys? Surely these are old cars being driven with due deference to their age and value by people who would be driving something modern if they had real talent. That's very wide of the mark. Naturally there are wealthy owners with limited abilities, but the overall standard is high; and very high at the front of the grids.

Martin Stretton is a good example. From the big Lagonda in race one he jumped into the smaller supercharged 1932 Maserati 4CM to give another stunning demonstration against Peter Hannen in his newer 1937 6CM Maserati in the Pre 1952 GP race. Stretton had been on pole but by Stowe on lap three Hannen was through into the lead, prompting Stretton to spectacular efforts. On one pass the cars touched at Luffield.

The following lap Hannen had Stretton first along one side then the other before he was though at Luffield, storming away with an 85.8mph fastest lap before coasting to a halt on the last lap. What happened? 'The car was running warm even to begin with, so I wanted to get ahead, and create enough of a gap so the car could cool down; but steam was coming out of the bonnet on the last lap so I stopped. I hope it's nothing serious.'

Stretton and the 4CM would be back the next day, even though all hope of the aggregate win had obviously gone. This clearly showed the worth of the two-race format. Stretton had time to find out what was wrong with the Maserati and fix it. 'The radiator split yesterday,' he explained, 'and the water caused it to misfire, so I just switched off.'

Not finishing the first race meant a start from the back of the 34-car grid on Sunday – which simply provided some even more spectacular driving as he cut through the whole field. Midway through the first lap he was up to fifth. For just a few moments the crowd enjoyed the glorious sight of a red Alfa P3 in the lead before Sir John Venables-Llewelyn was swallowed up by Peter Hannen's Maserati, only for the storming Stretton to pass Hannen too, at Stowe on only the second lap. From there, Stretton gave one of the most outstanding displays of the whole weekend. The front wheels were constantly twitching but never off line with the car extravagantly tail-out through the corners but never quite enough to run out of lock, and always in total control. Stretton used every inch of the track and more, but even with a wheel off the road never looked in the least trouble.

Stretton had treated the spectators to something similar in the second part of the Pre War Sports Car race which started Sunday's meeting. His display there led Klaus Werner to call him the 'Michael Schumacher of vintage racing' as he outbraked the Alfa going down Hangar Straight, and outdrove the faster car before handing over to Amanda who nevertheless had to give best to Peter Groh for the aggregate win.

Outstanding though they were, there was more to the racing than Martin Stretton's displays, although he inevitably won the Driver of the Day award. You won't find many more determined drivers than Mark Hales, Frank Sytner or Barrie Williams and they were all in action in the two-part GT Race where a brace of AC Cobras were up against nine Ferraris (including two GTOs and two 250 SWBs), a flock of Lotus Elites, five Astons and five E-types. The action was set to come from one Aston and one E-type in particular. Hales was lead driver in the 1962 Aston Martin Project 214 with Barrie Williams setting off in Nigel Corner's famous silver lightweight E-type. It didn't take long at all for Hales to leave his braking just a fraction too late while chasing Williams into Brooklands. The nose of the Aston slipped neatly under the back of the E-type, lifting it just far enough off the ground for a lurid tyre-smoking spin to be inevitable, but for

Right: superb field for the GT Race. Winning E-type of Williams and Corner is on far right, just behind leading Aston Project 214

Third place in the GT Race, behind the Jaguar and the Aston, went to the Ferrari 275GTB/C of Sytner and Pearson, right

Ham's Lister Jaguar, right, closes in on Bennett's gorgeous Aston Martin DB3S in the Louis Vuitton 1950s Sports Car Race

once Williams was the innocent party.

He was almost instantly back under control, across the grass, onto the track in pursuit of Hales and soon to be past him. He then put on the same sort of display of stunning car control we'd seen from Stretton, even hanging the tail out coming in for the obligatory driver change, having set a fastest lap of 86.7mph. Team mate Nigel Corner took the car home to an easy win ahead of the Aston, with Sytner back in third in the 275 GTB-C.

Williams and Sytner were soon back in action for the Louis Vuitton 1950s Sports Car Race, with Sytner in his element in the JCB D-type against the likes of Gary Pearson in the knobbly Lister and Tony Dron in the Salvadori/Shelby Le Mans-winning Aston DBR1 - with Shelby himself watching the performance. Sytner was soon through into second place ahead of Williams, and pressuring Pearson so hard in Luffield he almost lost it.

Williams then spun off after overtaking Sytner, who also lost places in the avoiding action required but was soon past Dron and back on the case despite nearly spinning in Becketts and getting it sideways through Woodcote. By the end of lap six he was right on Pearson's tail but his race effectively ended on the last lap at Brooklands. Sytner tried to take avoiding action but glanced off the side of Mason-Styrron's spinning Maserati on to the grass. It was a typically determined Sytner performance, repeated with a similar lack of success on Sunday when Pearson's Lister won again after the team had been up until the early hours replacing the head gasket.

The Hales/Williams incident from the GT race was the amusing side; the cars were battle scarred rather than damaged, and ready to go again on Sunday. The other side of the coin came in Saturday's fourth event, the pre 1960 GP race. Already stopped once when Phil Walker's Lotus spread gravel over the track through running wide, it was red-flagged for a far more serious incident. Rick Hall had just taken the lead from Walker when his Connaught ran wide at Club. Hall struggled with the car, almost bouncing right out of it as he wears no safety belts. At one point the car dug its front wheel into the ground with the back rearing into the air. For a moment it looked as though it might go end over end before it fell back, breaking the left rear suspension as it hit the kerb, out of control and veering across the track just in

Right, a stirring sight in the pre-1952 Grand Prix Car Race, with two Alfa Romeo 8C Monzas battling in the mid-field

Right, Amanda Stretton gets to grips with the 1936 Lagonda in the Pre-War Sports Car Race

Left, Tony Merrick was going very quickly indeed in the Ferrari 246 Dino, chasing Walker's Lotus 16 all the way to the line

The featured Coys marque, left, was MG. Simply glorious eight-cylinder Alfa Monoposto, far left

time to catch his son Rob Hall in the chasing BRM P25. Neither was hurt; both cars were seriously damaged.

The Halls' view was from the philosophical 'accidents will happen' school but the fact is that gravel traps designed for modern Formula One cars do not suit drifting classics. Without the gravel, the Connaught would have carried on over the grass and rejoined without harm but you can hardly redesign the track any more than the organisers had already done to suit what's competing on any given weekend.

Sadly the incidents made something of a mockery of a potentially great race – which in the end faced a third restart for just a three-lap sprint. At the finish Phil Walker's Lotus was still in the lead but the Lotus 16's legendary unreliablity was put to a better test in the second part of the race on the Sunday. Then it was given a really hard time by Tony Merrick's ex-Fangio Ferrari 246 Dino, which needed to win from Walker by a few seconds to get the aggregate victory and was quickly past pole man Walker. It took Walker six laps to catch and find a way past, at Bridge, but it had already been clear that the Dino was much more of a handful than the smaller and far more agile Lotus and Merrick's comment at the end summed it up: 'Hard work' was about all he could utter.

Third was the beautiful but utterly unsuccessful American Scarab, a front-engined GP car built just in time for F1 to go rear-engined. American owner/driver Don Orosco felt the same about Silverstone as the Germans: 'Lovely circuit. A flat track and bright sunshine; it's just like California'. But even at Laguna Seca, and for all the spectacle of the cars going down through the Corkscrew, you won't see racing like this.

Nor will you see such a mouthwatering array of cars both on and off the track. If you didn't bother to watch a single race you could still see more classics than you're ever likely to see together anywhere else. The

Coys Festival always attracts the car clubs and they were all here once again. Where else would you see seven Isos together, as many Panteras or a dozen Alpine A110s, not to mention just about every AC you can imagine – with real Cobras surprisingly happy to rub shoulders with dozens of fake snakes. The atmosphere is so good, no one seems in the least judgemental.

And easily outdoing all the club displays was MG, this year's featured marque. The invitational concours had 50 cars divided into 13 classes to show the whole history of MG. It included the oldest surviving MG, the 1928 14/40 and three supercharged K3 Magnettes, but it was far more than a static display; a 42-car grid had been assembled for perhaps the biggest MG race of all time, designed to be more than a procession.

Stirling Moss was there, 66 years old and driving an ex-works B, the Autosport championship winner of 1963. Against him were other noted MG exponents Barry Sidery-Smith and Colin Pearcy. Moss's initial lead soon faded away as Sidery-Smith and Pearcy went at it hammer and tongs, Pearcy's lightweight (relatively) MGC GTS holding off every extravagantly sideways move from Sidery-Smith's Le Mans B despite waving a front wheel in the air when really pressed through the tighter corners. Pearcy admitted afterwards that it was very hard work: 'MGCs were built for long distance events like the Sebring 12 Hours, not for sprinting around here, and it was a bit of a handful. It just doesn't want to go around corners like Luffield.'

After a while sensory overload sets in. At the end you would have seen 15 races with cars from as early as 1928 to as late as 1972, from cars as humble as Hillman Imps in the Historic Saloon Car Race to ones as exotic as the GTOs and as powerful as the GT40s and Lola T70s in the pre 1972 Le Mans class. There's far more than you can absorb; the only solution is to go back again next year, as most of this crowd most surely will.

BMW 328

Sixty years on

In 1996, one of the greatest of all sports cars celebrated its 60th anniversary. The BMW 328 made its debut as war clouds were gathering - but even before the war, the 328 had rewritten the racing record books. And after it, it rose again.
CHRIS WILLOWS *traces its remarkable career*

A ll around Europe, 1936 brought clear signals of approaching conflict. Hitler retook the Rhineland, Franco seized power in Spain, Mussolini announced the anti-communist Axis. In England, Edward VIII was proclaimed King, only to abdicate within a year. Already, the propaganda machine of the Nazi state was using all means at its disposal to demonstrate its superiority. Yet, even now, few bar those of Churchillian persuasion foresaw the havoc about to be visited upon Europe; and beneath the clamour of the world stage, life - and sport - went on much as normal.

Germany had its successes. Black athlete Jesse Owens rather embarrassed the Hitler regime by winning four gold medals at the Munich Olympics; but in a different sport, the state-backed Auto Union and Mercedes Grand Prix teams won most of the major 750kg formula races - demonstrating not so much the Aryan supremacy that Hitler intended as the fact that he who has the biggest budget wins. Much as today, in fact.

The Briem and Richter 328 in the 1940 Mille Miglia. They finished fifth, but it was a coupe that won

*BMW's 315/1
and 319/1
were the 328's
sporting pre-
decessor, and
equally at
home on an
English trials
course as on a
race track*

Elsewhere, wealthy amateurs competed at venues as diverse as Brooklands, Le Mans, Shelsley Walsh and the Mille Miglia, for the spirit of competition and the glow of success. Then, on 14 June 1936, news from Germany may have alerted such enthusiasts to a new sports car which was to create a legend.

On that date, the BMW 328 made its debut, at the Eifelrennen meeting on the Nurburgring. And although still lacking doors, the all-white 328 prototype, with its shapely body, faired-in wings and purposeful gait, made its rivals look old hat.

It went even better than it looked. Ernst Henne, sometime Mercedes Grand Prix driver and motorcycle land speed record holder, drove the 'white arrow' in the 2-litre sports racing class. He completed the five-lap race at an average of 63.4mph, three minutes ahead of his nearest class rival, two-and-a-half minutes in front of the more powerful supercharged Alfas and Bugattis.

On the day, not all the amateurs welcomed a 'works' car, unavailable to the public, into their sporting preserve. Within months, however, the 328 was offered for sale, complete with doors, and thereafter, if you wanted to win, you had to have one. From 1937 the 2-litre sports car class became BMW territory.

The company had been formed 20 years earlier, as a manufacturer of aero engines, and had rapidly acquired a reputation for good design and excellent performance at high altitudes. When this avenue of engineering was cut off to German companies by the Versailles Treaty, BMW designed its first motorcycle and involved itself in competition to prove the worth of its machines.

By 1928, when BMW made the move into car production, by acquiring Fahrzeugfabrik Eisenach, its two-wheelers had won countless trials, races and speed records. Fahrzeugfabrik Eisenach, however, was the maker of the tiny but popular Dixi car -which was actually an Austin Seven built under licence! BMW quickly modified it into its own first four-wheeler, the 3/15, and as with the motor cycles, soon went racing. In 1929, the company entered a team of three 3/15s in the Internationale Alpenfahrt - an event featuring Rudolf Caracciola, Felice Nazzaro and one Alfred Neubauer, all accomplished international racers. The team ran like clockwork and won the gold cup for best team performance.

But having tasted both commercial and sporting success with its small car, BMW hankered after bigger and better things. The former head of the motorcycle division, a gifted engineer named Rudolf Schleicher, rejoined BMW from Horch in 1930 and developed its first six-cylinder car engine - which made its debut in the 1182cc BMW 303 in 1933. The six-cylinder layout echoed the configuration of the company's early aero engines and has remained a passion for BMW engineers ever since.

Within a year, a 34bhp 1490cc version powered the 315, followed in 1935 by the 45bhp 1.9-litre 319. Both were offered with saloon or cabriolet coachwork, and BMW completed the family with its first six-cylinder sports cars - roadster versions of the 315 and 319, each accorded the designation -/1.

Higher compression, three sidedraft Solex carburettors and a new intake manifold boosted output to 40 and 55bhp respec-

tral plugs. A layman unbuckling the leather bonnet straps to look for the first time at a 328 engine might assume it to be a double overhead camshaft unit with downdraft carbs feeding the cylinders: but herein lies the ingenuity of the design. In reality, the chain-driven camshaft remains buried in the block, and long pushrods operate the inlet valves. Rocker arms on the inlet side then actuate shorter, horizontal pushrods which cross the vee to operate the exhaust valves. Coil and distributor ignition were state-of-the-art for a 1930s sports car and in standard form, with 7.5:1 compression, the 328 engine produced 80bhp at 5000rpm - a tremendous output from a production 2-litre of 60 years ago.

Meanwhile Schleicher and another Horch recruit, Fritz Fiedler, refined the chassis too. The wheelbase and track of the A-frame ladder chassis remained unchanged as did the suspension layout, hydraulic dampers and direct, accurate rack and pinion steering. However, larger brakes were housed within the 16-inch disc wheels and, importantly, now featured hydraulic actuation.

The body retained the sleek look of the 319/1 but was at once both more elegant and purposeful - with tall, narrow kidney

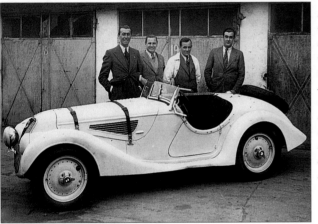

In 1936, the works cars, on loan to AFN, won team prize in the TT at Ards. In March 1938, Lurani, Schaumburg-Lippe, Loof and Fane pose with a 328 before the Mille Miglia

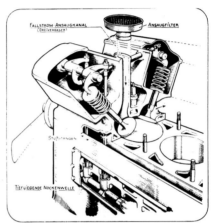

The 328 engine's valve gear was a masterpiece of design, its clever crossover pushrod layout allowing inclined valves and hemispherical combustion chambers even with just a single, in-block camshaft

tively, while the light, rigid tubular chassis allowed the independent front suspension and live rear axle to do their job. The neat roadster shape eschewed the vintage tradition of a 'torpedo' body with separate mudguards, in favour of front and rear wings which flowed into the main body, with rear wheels enclosed by stylish spats. And the way that the 315/1's tail tapered down to a point where it joined the wings gave a clear promise of speed.

The 315/1 made its sporting debut in the 1934 International Alpine Rally and the team's performance attracted envious glances from its 1.5-litre rivals, not least Fraser Nash. That marque had won previous Alpines with its famous 'chain gang' cars but in 1934 the Aldington brothers received a sound drubbing at the hands of BMW. Not only did the light German cars have plenty of go, but their handling and manoeuvrability made the Nashes look like the vintage cars they were. The Aldingtons quickly recognised both a better design and a promising business opportunity; by 1935 AFN had secured the BMW agency for the United Kingdom and the cars were to be called, and badged, Frazer Nash-BMWs. If you can't beat them. . .

Then as now, sound evolution was a core BMW philosophy, and steady development of the six-cylinder engine plus the light, wieldy 319/1 chassis led inexorably to the 328. Schleicher increased the bore of the 1911cc engine by 1mm to achieve a capacity of 1971cc. He concluded that the head design restricted breathing, and so produced an aluminium alloy head with hemispherical combustion chambers, valves in vee formation, and cen-

The 328 engine could easily be mistaken for a twin overhead camshaft unit with downdraft carburettors in the vee between the 'camshafts' - which are really rocker shafts!

Nurburgring 1938, the 2-litre sportscar race was won by Greifzu's 328 number 10. Shelsley 1938, Paul Heinemann is in a 328

grilles, headlamps neatly integrated into the valleys 'twixt bonnet and wings, and an altogether more harmonious tail design, 10cm longer than its forebear. Weighing around 830kg, the 328 was capable of nearly 100mph and its long-stroke engine delivered lots of torque low down, making it an easy car to drive swiftly.

Its Nurburgring debut win presaged a fine international career. Minor problems excluded the team cars from the French GP (then for sports cars) but in September the works 328s were lent to AFN for the Tourist Trophy, at Ards in Ulster. All three were painted dark green and they easily took the team prize, with A J P Fane winning the 2-litre class and finishing third overall.

For 1937, deliveries of customer cars began and result sheets grew thick with 328 victories. Many were private cars but at events of major prestige BMW rolled out the works team. The record book for 1937 shows class or outright wins in the Monte Carlo rally, the Eifel races, the GP of Bucharest, the Tourist Trophy again, and success at hill climbs like La Turbie, Shelsley Walsh and in the German hill climb championship. In April one

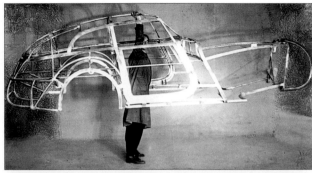

What's under the skin of one of the 1940 Munich-built 328 coupes

Touring Coupe leads open 328 at Le Mans in 1939. Coupe finished fifth

of the first 'doorless' 328s was prepared by AFN for an hour's blind at Brooklands, with S C H 'Sammy' Davis at the helm. This 'standard' 328 running on pump petrol covered 102.22 miles in the hour, a fantastic performance which established a new record.

Success continued into 1938 with notable class victories in the 24-hour race at Spa-Francorchamps and in the Mille Miglia (where 328s finished eighth and tenth behind larger, more powerful opposition). The engineering team, however (now under Ernst Loof), saw that there was little development left in the larger Alfa Romeo, Delage and Delahaye sports cars: so perhaps with intensive work the 328 could fight for overall victory, despite the handicap of its smaller engines. Lighter rocker arms, con rods, pushrods, dural tappets and electron alloy pistons were tried, to reduce weight and increase engine speed. New cam profiles were developed, port and valve sizes grew and the carburettor venturis were reamed to enable more mixture to reach the cylinders. With compression up to 9.15:1, output reached 120bhp at 5700rpm - while even higher compression, lighter internals and a headier

fuel brew saw better than 130bhp - if only for very short periods!

One target BMW had in its sights was Le Mans. Not satisfied with a new engine alone, in March 1939 Loof sent a new 328 chassis to Carrozzeria Touring in Milan to be fitted with a lightweight body built to their unique Superleggera principle. The result was a spectacular, streamlined coupe shell mounted on a filigree tubular frame weighing just 35kg. The delightful 'teardrop' coupe finished fifth at La Sarthe, easily winning the 2-litre class at a pace which would have won outright in 1938, or indeed in 1949. Two normal 328s finished seventh and ninth, and as the goal of a major win came one step closer, BMW gritted its teeth for the final phase in the 328's development, or so it thought.

Loof authorised a series of 'home-built' 328 streamliners. Engineers Kempter, Meyerhuber and Huber used their own experience and that of Touring to develop a boxy coupe clearly influenced by the German school of aerodynamic design - of Paul Jaray, von Koenig-Fachsenfeld and Dr Wunibald Kamm. From this 'monster' came the classic 328 Mille Miglia roadster - a car as

Not all 328 streamliners were as neat as Touring's cars. This is a Wendler body on one of the early efforts

The 1940 Mille Miglia, sometimes called the Brescian Grand Prix, actually took place after the outbreak of war and the poster echoes the times. Brudes and Roese's 328 passes the race information board

pretty and delicate as the Munich coupe was ugly and ponderous, although testing proved the coupes to be faster (and the Munich-built car belied its appearance by exceeding 135mph).

So despite the onset of war, development continued unabated - with the aim of competing in the 1940 Mille Miglia, scheduled for 28 April on a triangular 103-mile course linking Brescia, Cremona and Mantua. Nine laps of fast, straight roads linked by hairpin corners was not the customary Brescia-Rome-Brescia event route, but the 927-mile endurance race would test engine, chassis and brakes in equal measure.

BMW took two coupes and three of the svelte, lightweight spyders which so neatly presaged the Jaguar XK120. Facing them were four 2.5-litre 6C2500SS Alfa coupes, two Delages and the Avio 815 - Enzo Ferrari's first car, on its debut. The larger Alfas were favourites to win but after practice it was clear that the BMWs had an advantage. All five used identical 120bhp racing engines, the weight of the coupes being about 780kg and the roadsters 700kg. And despite their 25 per cent larger engines, the Alfas could not overcome their 300kg weight penalty.

The Touring Coupe driven by Huschke von Hanstein and Walter Baumer led all the way, with the Munich coupe of Count 'Johnny' Lurani and Franco Cortese running second before retiring. The 328 spyders were also quicker than the Alfas but, delayed by slower pitwork, they finished third, fifth and sixth. The winning car averaged 104.2mph over eight hours 54 minutes, creating for BMW an indelible place in history and writing the final chapter in this extraordinary sports car's works record.

Farina's Alfa Romeo finished 15 minutes behind the winner - drawing on itself the wrath of the Italian media, who mocked that in the meantime the BMW could have driven to Milan. So BMW went home with overall victory, the team prize and the lap record, a fitting finale for the 328, which was due to gain a new twin camshaft engine for 1941, with the later prospect of fuel injection, which BMW also had under development.

All this, of course, was lost as the war dragged into its second year; but in fact the NSKK (a sporting arm of the Nazi party which had entered the three MM roadsters) continued to develop the 328 with an even lighter Touring body for the proposed Berlin-Rome race in 1941. The race never took place and the car didn't appear in public until 1996, when in further celebration of the 328's 60th birthday, it took part in the Mille Miglia, the Goodwood Festival of Speed and the Monterey historic races.

But even the war didn't mark the end of the 328 story. Not by some way. After it, BMW's car production facility at Eisenach sat a few kilometres inside the new East German border and was commandeered by the communists. Back in West Germany the large and heavily bombed Munich factory, which would have produced aero engines had it not been almost inoperable, was under the control of the allies, who ordered the facility to be dismantled.

As the company struggled to survive (making pots, pans and bicycles out of aero engine cylinders and other scrap material), its former car plant resumed production of pre-war BMWs. The company was Eisenacher Motoren Werke and the Eastern BMWs became EMWs, sporting a quartered white and red

The BMW team cars at Brescia in 1940, and Brudes and Roese on their way to third place in that Mille Miglia

badge, plagiarising the famous white and blue of BMW proper.

The Aldingtons (of AFN) meanwhile used RAF connections to visit old friends at the Munich factory and reclaim H J's 328, crashed at a race in Hamburg shortly before the declaration of war. And although he could find no trace of his own car he did see one of the 1940 Mille Miglia roadsters, which he claimed and drove back to England over the ravaged roads of Europe. With a Frazer Nash grille, it was shown to the press as the new post-war Frazer Nash - from which sprang the famous Le Mans Replica,

Sebring and Targa Florio models, and even a single-seater.

Fortuitously for AFN, given the problem of finding suitable engines to power such cars, the Aldingtons had also brought back plans for the six-cylinder 328 engine (which in different tune also powered the 327) and convinced the Bristol aero engine company to produce it. Bristol in its turn, seeking to make up for depleted revenue from its aero engine business, wanted to start building complete cars. Don Aldington procured the 327 coupe, commended it to Bristol as the ideal basis for a gentleman's luxury carriage, and bingo, the Bristol 400 was born, as a quality car which perfectly complemented the more overtly sporting FNs.

At the same time, the Bristol-built 328 engine - vastly improved with post-war metallurgy - grew ever more powerful in successive versions to the point where the Le Mans Bristol 450 and Cooper-Bristol F2 cars could boast 150bhp and more, leading the 328 legend towards yet another era, as motor sport edged towards post-war revival.

Now, carefully hidden 328s emerged from nooks and crannies around Europe; and even though their owners faced seemingly insurmountable problems in finding fuel, tyres and spares, the sport began slowly to find its feet, and then to flourish again. Pre-war cars were rebuilt, fettled, then raced just as they were six to eight years before. Again, the same designs proved successful.

Ernst Loof formed Veritas and turned 328s into sleek, lightweight single seaters and sports cars. Veritas and sister marque AFM, built by Alex von Falkenhausen (BMW's pre-war motorcycle engineer and later Chief Engineer) dominated German events well into the 1950s, while (following BMW's successful protection of its trademark) the EMWs from the East became AWEs from Automobilwerk Eisenach.

With twin-cam heads on the familiar 328 block, such cars raced at very high speed circuits such as Avus, the Grenzlandring (near Aachen) and Montlhery, and it says much for the pace of these highly modified BMW units that they lapped the Grenzlandring road circuit faster than cars were lapping the Indianapolis oval in the same year.

The list of victories and places for these varied progeny of

the 328 would fill a book. In one heat of the 1950 Monza F2 GP Hans Stuck outran the works Ferrari team in his AFM. Le Mans, Chimay, Nurburgring, Freiburg, Solitude, Berne, the Targa Florio and many, many more would all appear on the roll. A 328 won the 1952 Alpine rally outright, while the Bristol engine, notably in the AC Ace, extended the 328's life into the early 1960s - 25 years after it had made such an impact at the Nurburgring. BMW itself, when it finally managed to return to automobile manufacture in 1952, even resorted to a version of the 1971cc six to power its 'Baroque Angel', the 501.

Just 462 examples of the 328 were built during its brief production life from 1937 to 1940. Yet the soundness of its design philosophy and its widespread influence after its own career finished have bestowed upon it a legendary status. Little wonder that in so many great car collections, nestling amongst the Ferraris, Maseratis and Alfa Romeos will sit a Frazer Nash Le Mans Replica, an AC Ace or maybe even a real 328.

PROGRESS IS OUR GOAL

TRADITION IS OUR SOUL.

BMW Mobile Tradition
BMW AG commitment in the areas:

Historical vehicle collection
Historical documentation
BMW Museum
Workshop for historical BMW vehicles
Parts sales for historical BMW vehicles
BMW Clubs

BMW Mobile Tradition
Petuelring 130
80788 Munich

SHEER DRIVING PLEASURE.

9-11 AUGUST
Oldtimer, Nurburgring

Just occasionally, the classic racing scene resembles the modern Grand Prix circus, and August is a good example. From the Coys Historic Festival, many of the cars go virtually straight to the Nurburgring, for the Oldtimer GP the following weekend. Sadly, though, the Oldtimer is not the event it used to be and perhaps Coys is partly to blame; after all, it isn't everyone who has the resources to do two large events back to back.

But although the atmosphere this time was a bit flatter than normal, there were some compensations. Just as Silverstone had a new track configuration for the historics at the Coys Festival, at the Nurburgring the cars were using the full Grand Prix circuit for the first time. That still may not have the allure and mystique of the old 'Ring, but nonetheless it drew a crowd of getting on for 60,000 to watch almost 500 drivers.

And none of them should have any great complaints about the scope and variety of the races. There was everything from early-perpendicular Edwardians, like Jean-Louis Duret's wonderful 1906 Alco, Mark Walker's all-engine 1913 Monarch and Graham Rankin's 1906 Fiat, to several rather more recent Porsche 956s. Nearly all the 24 Edwardian cars had come over from Britain and once again the British entries accounted for a large proportion of many of the race entries.

The Oldtimer is a long weekend; it has to be to fit all the action in, starting with a 500km sports car race on the Thursday

The Scarabs have been doing the rounds this year and one turned up for the August Oldtimer. This Delahaye 135, right, rejoined battle with the various Bentleys and Alfas of the 1930s

where the brawn of the Steve Hitchin AC Cobra was too much for the Brendon Wang 250LM Ferrari, shared by Gary Pearson and Paul Alexander and which expired before the finish, as did other challengers like John Beasley's Cooper Monaco which he was sharing with Peter Hannen.

Retirements are hardly the end of the world in these sort of events: so many drivers are involved in so many races that there's always another opportunity to shine, and Gary Pearson did not have long to wait. Helped by the rugged reliability of the Lister Jaguar that had already just won at Silverstone, he came out on top in both rounds of the Louis Vuitton sports car races on the Saturday and Sunday.

Inescapably that gave him the aggregate win and although Jeffrey Pattinson, the series leader, managed a second and third that was not even enough for the aggregate runners up spot - which went to Tony Dron driving magnificently in the Aston Martin DBR1. Just as at Silverstone Barrie Williams had a mechanical glitch to contend with. After third place in Saturday's race his Tojeiro Jaguar blew a head gasket the following day.

The Oldtimer, like Coys, is a good excuse for the top drivers to show their impressive versatility. Just as Martin Stretton had shone in virtually everything at Silverstone, Pearson now showed what he could do, going on to add a win in the first round of the European Historic F2 race in a Tecno. It helped that Rob Hall was stopped with a puncture but Pearson had still come from the fourth row and contended with a wet track to win.

Puncture fixed, Hall resumed his rightful place by winning the Sunday round ahead of Fredy Kumschick's Lotus 69, as Pearson slipped back to fifth. He must have been well pleased; his puncture in the first race had come right on top of his crash the previous week at Silverstone, so he was ready for a change of luck.

Mark Walter's 1913 Monarch, above, was one of the 24 Edwardians over from the UK. Roberto Radaelli gave the rare Zagato-bodied 1954 Alfa Romeo 1900 an airing

Burkhard von Schenk appeared in suitably period headgear to drive the 1957 Porsche 550 Spider

As for Stretton, it would be an unusual meeting indeed if he didn't demonstrate his talent convincingly and he must have amazed European spectators by showing just what the unlikely looking 1936 4.5-litre Lagonda could do on the Nurburgring - impressing much as he had at Silverstone.

This time he had to give best to a pair of Alfas, the two Monzas, of Klaus Werner (his opponent from Silverstone) and Hein Gericke but then you might reasonably expect the GP cars to have the edge over a Le Mans endurance racer. . .

Far nearer the top of the card in power and performance, the International SuperSports Cup was also a double-header, with 34 cars fighting it out. The might of Charlie Agg's McLaren M8F was seriously challenged by the other M8F of Richard Eyre who won the Saturday round. Unfortunately for Eyre, he could only win by the tightest of margins, 0.8 sec and with Agg winning by five seconds the following day the aggregate win was just Agg's.

Predictably the two Porsche 956s were too much for older opposition like Jonathan Baker's Lola T70 in the newly introduced race for 'recent' Le Mans cars, but Baker still managed a fine second place as one of the 956s, that of Christophe Bouchut, managed to account for the other, driven by Lars Jonsson, when that one was leading. Jonsson was apparently so taken aback that he could only manage fifth the following day, although this time Bouchet had no trouble in winning by over half a minute.

The Type 22 Bugatti still goes fast enough to make most people wear a helmet - but Angela Hucke, above, seems unperturbed. A Lister, right, awaits the start of the Louis Vuitton sports car race

Blackhawk COLLECTION

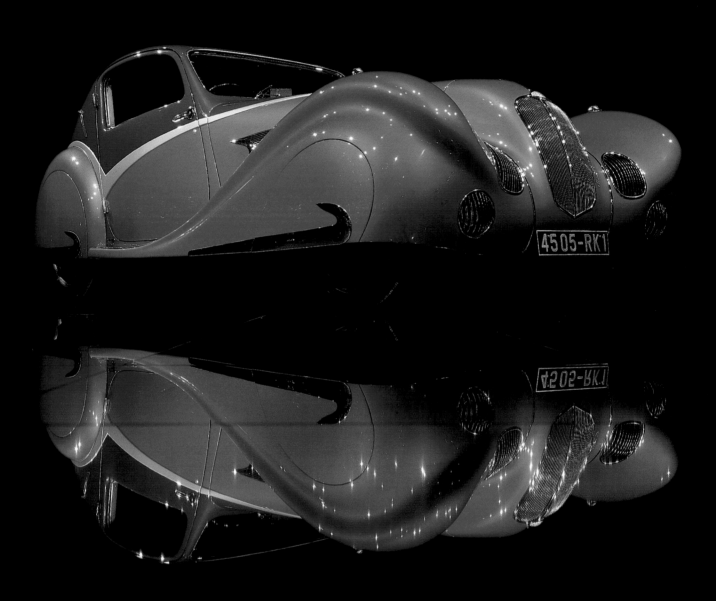

4505-RK1

Purveyors of Rolling Art

For inquiries regarding buying or selling of American or European Classic Cars
and Custom Coachwork or One-of-a-kind Automobiles, please contact

BLACKHAWK COLLECTION
3600 BLACKHAWK PLAZA CIRCLE,
DANVILLE, CALIFORNIA 94506-3600 U.S.A.
Telephone (510) 736-3444   Facsimile (510) 736-4375

A long way from Brooklands but the right crowd and no crowding, for practice at least

Monterey

There is no more car obsessed culture anywhere in the world than that of California, and no more comprehensive celebration of classic motoring than the annual combination of Pebble Beach Concours and Laguna Seca races. BRIAN LABAN commuted from seashore to circuit

In the third weekend of August on the Monterey Peninsula, south of San Francisco, deep in Steinbeck country, you can positively wallow in nostalgia. If your taste is for perfection on a pedestal you can head for the most glamorous of all concours, at Pebble Beach. Or if you prefer memories spiced with action, you'll find one of the world's great historic race meetings at nearby Laguna Seca, high in the California hills near Carmel.

In Carmel Valley on Friday, the front nine holes of the Quail Lodge golf course host the delightfully relaxed Concours Italiano, while for those with money to spare and a motor house to fill there's the five-day Blackhawk Collection sale, or auctions by Christie's and US specialist Rick Cole, all just bursting at the seams with serious temptations.

The weekend fills every bar and restaurant with racing talk, every parking lot with classics. Between Pebble Beach and Laguna you will see more spectacular cars on any country backroad than you might normally see in a lifetime.

It's a petrolhead party weekend and it starts early, with the Concours Italiano, where, for one afternoon, Quail Lodge becomes a sea of red machinery on the green fairways, surrounded by the white tents of autojumble and merchandising stalls. There was an Italian fashion show too, and a tribute to the designs of Nuccio Bertone, featuring a fine collection of concept cars, including both Alfa Romeo BAT car

and futuristic Stratos prototype. De Tomaso was an appropriate choice for featured marque, given its preference for big US V8s, and you could hardly move for Lamborghinis, Alfas and Maseratis. There were at least a hundred Ferraris, and probably as many Italian picnics. . .

The annual Blackhawk 'Exposition' is on another golf course, a couple of long iron shots from the Pebble Beach arena, in the pine forests by Carmel Bay and the blue Pacific. It isn't quite a concours and it isn't quite an auction: more the world's most exclusive used car lot. It looks like a motor museum in a small village of marquees, but the Blackhawk Collection is really a constantly changing inventory of top-of-the-market classics, with a permanent base in Danville, California, and a travelling schedule which takes it from America to Europe and Japan, to show and to sell cars.

And not any old cars. Here, Blackhawk offered around 70 classics, from 1937 Adler competition coupe (ex Le Mans, 1937 and 1938) to 1950 Talbot Lago Veth & Zoon cabriolet (third in class just down the road last year). Those and the cars in between (Alfa, Auburn, Bentley, Bugatti, Delahaye, Duesenberg, Ferrari, Hispano, Lincoln, Mercedes, Packard and Rolls, to name but a few) had a total list price of more than $45 million. You do not need a calculator to figure that that means an average of more than half a million dollars a car. This is definitely not your typical used car showroom. . .

Looking is free, and literally thousands do. Buying is expensive, but in recent years Blackhawk has sold more than a few previous Pebble Beach winners, and probably a few future ones. Tempt you to a 1930 'Grosser' Mercedes-Benz 770K Cabriolet sir? Call it $4 million. Something more sporty? How about a Porsche 908-02 Spyder, formerly owned and raced by Steve McQueen, second overall in the Sebring 12-Hour, and camera car for the film Le Mans during the 1970 race. We'll negotiate, but say $950,000? A 1938 Talbot Lago 150SS with Teardrop coupe body by Figoni et Falaschi; two million? A 1931 Murphy bodied 8-litre Bentley - exquisite at $1.25 million. Or if you want to be really serious about this, this lovely 1931 Bugatti Royale Binder Coupe de Ville, $12.5 million. Yes, $12.5 million. . .

You can spot the potential buyers by their warm glow of wealth, but they aren't looking down on the families under their feet with Hawaiian shirts, Beanie hats and candy-coated kids. Americans are more relaxed about life than some Europeans.

On Friday at Laguna, as the paddock filled, we saw a large motorhome with a couple of open-wheelers in front of it. A very big, very American woman under the awning pointed a camera at a four-year-old kid on a pedal car. 'Ohhh Kaaay!', she whoops, 'let's see how FAST you can go!' A sound attitude.

1950s Ferraris warm up alongside '70s Can-Am McLarens and '80s Grand Prix cars. There's a whole stable of late '60s Trans-Am cars in one row. A 1967 Mercury Cougar, ex Dan Gurney; Smoky Yunick's R/T Racing '69 Mustang; Dick Thomson's '66 Mustang. They start the Cougar and leave its 4.8 V8 at a fast idle to warm through. Its massive off-beat rumble makes the ground move. It sounds like an over-amplified drum solo from a bad rock band. When they start the two Mustangs, the noise is so intense and the fuel fumes so pungent we actually have to move.

You could be churlish and call the event parochial. The vast majority of entries is from the USA, and predominantly from California and neighbouring states. Of best part of 400 cars, less than 25 are listed as being from outside North America - mostly from Germany, given this year's BMW celebration, plus the UK, Australia and New Zealand, Singapore, Japan, Mexico, Argentina and Canada. You would spot a lot more drivers who are no more American than I am, but for the organisers, either they live here or the car does, so the entry is American. Stirling Moss? Hanover, New Hampshire; Brian Redman? Hermosa Beach, California; Robs Lamplough? Rancho Santa Fe, California; Tony Merrick? Emeryville, California. You get the picture.

But just as the USA and California are home to most of the world's roadgoing exotica, so are they where classic racing cars come to retire. The variety and quality of cars at Laguna are remarkable. Cars remembered from photographs, from race reports, from actual races - in the metal, in oh-so-familiar livery, and racing again just as they should be in their advancing years.

Drivers, too. Almost the first face we saw at the track this morning was American hero Sam Posey's. Then Nelson Piquet, Redman, Bill Morton, Bob Akin, Moss, Phil Hill, George Follmer, Vic Edelbrock, Kenper Miller, Marc Surer, Dieter Quester. If you know motor racing history, you'll know them all.

You might also hear that it isn't real racing at Laguna Seca, because organiser Steve Earle and his sanctioning body the Historic Motor Sports Association have a 'nannying' attitude towards cars and drivers. It doesn't come across. HMSA's 'Statement of Purpose' is 'to encourage the restoration, preservation and use of historic sports and racing cars'. To HMSA 'restore'

Bugattis in the sunshine, above. Ex-pat Brit Murray Smith in his ex-Andretti Lotus, left, described the Corkscrew as 'like driving out of an open window'

means to bring back to former condition, not to make new.

They emphasise originality: only modifications (and wheels and tyres) that could have appeared on the car in its racing career are permissible; only historically correct markings are acceptable, modern advertising isn't. Hence the familiarity. One spectating European racer suggested that the circuit was 'technical', for which read basically easy. Murray Smith, on the other hand, after his first practice in his newly acquired ex-Andretti Lotus 80, described driving hard through Laguna Seca's famous Corkscrew Turn as 'like driving out of an open window'.

And the HMSA rule that perhaps draws most scorn of all: 'Any driver in an accident sufficient to cause damage will be excluded from any future event. He may appeal his exclusion after one year's time'. Steve Earle himself was no doubt thinking all about that when he fell off with his McLaren M23. Tell a racing driver not to race? You must be joking. . .

Chrysler underlined their growing interest in the historic scene as main sponsor, but BMW was honoured marque and company and owners assembled a superb collection of cars for the BMW Salute on Saturday morning. Sixty years after the 328's Nurburgring debut there were dozens of 328s at Laguna, including the 1940 Mille Miglia roadster. There were 507s, and the first four 'art cars', painted by Alexander Calder, Frank Stella, Roy Lichtenstein and Andy Warhol, and each a Le Mans veteran. There was the 1979 March which won one of BMW's six F2 titles, hordes of 3.0 and 3.5CSL 'Batmobile' coupés, 1980s Group 4 and 5 M1s, M1 Procars, the Red Lobster IMSA car, the Brabham BT54 which followed Piquet's 1983 championship winning BT52, Junior Team 320s, a 1986 Benetton BMW-turbo F1 car - everything from an Isetta bubble car in Motorsport colours to this year's BMW-powered McLaren F1 GTR Le Mans

The Spirit of Brooklands, California style in Graham Wallis's 1929 Lagonda, right. Corkscrew Turn, below, just as it begins to flatten out!

Pebble Beach Concours d'Elegance

1948 BMW

Robert Pass
St. Louis
Missouri

Formula III
Veritas/Loof
Racer

The quieter side of the Monterey weekend, at Pebble Beach. Veritas racer, far left, fits in with Laguna's BMW theme. Classic lines, left, on 1933 Duesenberg J at Blackhawk expo

Attention to detail is only the final touch at Pebble, left. Japanese owned Testa Rossa rubs shoulders with older V12, from Lagonda

car. And more than one driver (not least Piquet in the GTR) seemed to think the exhibition laps were actually Race One.

The real racing was just that. Seven races on Saturday, seven on Sunday, featuring every age and shape of racing car. First winner was one of the invaders, Klaus Werner from Wuppertal, in a 1934 Alfa P3, holding off local man Tom Hollfender in a 1932 Alfa 8C2300 Monza and former world champion Phil Hill in his own 1932 Bugatti Type 54. Behind them were everything from Ford Specials to Maseratis and a 1938 Talbot Lago T26 SS, but Race Two made even that mix look ordinary. . .

It brought another German winner, Thomas Feierabend, and BMW's first win of the weekend - appropriately enough with a 328S. Frank Pritt's 1933 Alfa 8C-2300 was second, and there were four more 328s in the top ten. Behind them, at wildly differing paces, were such delights as a 1914 Mercer (which had 7 litres under the bonnet and sounded like it), a gaggle of Model T racers from 1914 to 1925 (tall and skinny wheeled, with one even boasting a riding mechanic), a tiny 750cc Austin 7 (snatching fourth place after battling wheel-to-wheel with a V12 Lagonda), and a three-wheeler Morgan taking on a mighty Indianapolis Duesenberg. Thirty starters and, incredibly, 28 happy finishers.

Robert Baker of Sun Valley, Idaho, won Saturday Race Three in his 1955 Porsche 550, and Don Racine livened up the list in third place in his 1952 850cc Aardvark. Race Four had former Grand Prix driver Pete Lovely in a 1959 250 Testarossa pressing Rob Walton's 1959 Maserati T-61 Birdcage at the front, ahead of Peter Shea's thundering 6.6-litre Ol' Yellar XI - the very image of a late '50s American sports racer showing its heels to assorted D-Types, Ferraris and more Birdcages.

Race Five saw assorted BMW 1600, 1800 and 2000Ti saloons ranged against Porsche, Lotus, Alfa and Ginetta sports

Quantum Sports Cars Tel. 01384 834422

Beauford Cars Ltd Tel. 01695 622608

Dakar Cars Tel. 01322 614044

L921 PAU

Gardner Douglas Tel. 01949 843299

AOY 300C

Hawk Cars Tel. 01892 750282 /341

NG TF

N G Cars Tel. 01372 748666

P412 DNN

Ultima Sports Ltd Tel. 01455 631366

Chesil Speedsters Tel. 01308 897072

HFO 432

M841 MOD

Marlin Engineering Tel. 01363 773772

Grinnall Cars Tel. 01299 822862

BRITISH BUILT - AND BACK ON TOP!

There's been many a tear shed at the demise of The Great British Motor Industry - but the future is looking very bright in the shape of the Association of Specialist Car Manufacturers - a group of leading British constructors committed to quality, and producing a wide choice of kits and complete hand built cars all designed and built in Britain.

Whether you prefer the irresistible curves of the Chesil Speedster, the aristocratic elegance of the Beauford, or the adrenalin - rush from driving the 600 bhp Ultima Sports - there's a car that's right for you.

If you want to be part of the resurgence in British car manufacturing, call us for a brochure and price list.

ASCM

ASSOCIATION OF SPECIALIST CAR MANUFACTURERS

cars, with Carmel resident Larry Menser taking the flag in his Porsche 904GTS ahead of two Japanese visitors, Junro Nishida in a Ginetta G12 and Shoji Tochibayashi in a Lotus 26R. And Race Six saw another gaggle of 2002Tis engulfed by the thunder of a huge gridful of Trans-Am monsters, before day one was rounded off by the 'modern' Grand Prix cars and a grid that would have done credit to many a real Grand Prix.

There were twenty starters (the oldest of them Quester's 1969 Dornier BMW F2, the most recent Steve Soper's BMW-turbo engined 1986 Benetton F1. There were five Shadows, three Marches, three McLarens, a couple of Williams, and one each of Brabham, Wolf, Lotus, Penske and BRM. Quester struggled to make the grid after electrical problems and survived only two laps, but BMW 'team-mate' Marc Surer gave the 3-litre F1 cars a very hard time with his 2-litre F2 March-BMW to finish a fighting second to Charles Nearburg's 1980 Williams FW07B. Murray Smith went the distance too, in 12th place, getting to grips with both the Corkscrew and the ex-Andretti Lotus 80, which is original even down to its green Martini paintwork. . .

On Sunday morning we detoured to the 46th Annual Pebble Beach Concours d'Elegance and quickly realised why Pebble has the reputation it does. The cars on the famous 18th fairway, a ribbon of green between Pebble Beach Lodge and the fringes of the bay, are stunning. This year's featured prewar marque (surprisingly, for the first time ever at Pebble Beach) was Lincoln and postwar star was coachbuilder Zagato.

Honorary judges this year included such luminaries as Lord Montagu, Gianpaolo Dallara, stylists Fabrizio Giugiaro, Bertone boss Paolo Caccamo, Chrysler's Tom Gale, Mercedes' Bruno Sacco, Andrea Zagato, Filippo Sapino of Ghia, GM's Wayne Cherry and Ford's Jack Telnak. The big brass were out too, headed by car-mad Chrysler boss Bob Lutz, both Jacques Nasser and Donald Petersen of Ford, and GM vice president Donald Runkle. Phil Hill, the first American world driver's champion (and him-self a Pebble Beach Best of Show winner in both 1955 and 1957) was on the list too, with another racing great, Denise McCluggage -probably America's greatest ever woman racer and now a highly respected motoring writer and columnist.

To them and the other judges fell the task of separating the cream from the cream in 25 classes and sub-classes from 'Antique through 1915' to 'Open Wheel Racers' - from a 1902 Mercedes 40hp Tourer to racers from GP Ferraris to Indianapolis roadsters. TV star Jay Leno was close with his streamlined 1934 Duesenberg J Walker Coupé (exquisitely presented after 60 years in storage!) and so were dozens of others but the Best of Show was deemed to be Sam and Emily Mann's gorgeous 1938 Delage D8-120 De Villars Cabriolet. Personally, I thought the real stars were the two Mormon Meteor Duesenberg record breakers driven by the legendary Ab Jenkins, and I have rarely heard anything like the aero-engined Meteor III idling through its Channel-tunnel sized exhaust; but then I'm just a sucker for racing cars. . .

And there were plenty more of those at Laguna on Sunday, for seven more races. Most were good, the last was the best, as Brian Redman ranged his 2-litre `Chevron B21-BMW against a grid with three GT40s (including one 7-litre Mk4) four Lola T70s, Ferrari 312 and 512Ps, two Alfa T33s, Panteras, Cobras, Porsches and a horde of BMWs which saw Piquet in the M1 Procar, Surer in his old 320, Morton, Miller and Posey in Batmobiles, Busby in a 320 Turbo and Quester in a Gp A 635.

Interrupted by the pace car for a couple of laps, it ran to 13 of the scheduled ten, as Redman clawed his way from tenth to the front with some truly incredible passes, several in the dramatic, falling, off-camber Corkscrew Turn. He passed Surer early on, then the flying Piquet, early leader Bert Skidmore's Lola T210, and finally, on the last lap with the crowd going wild, past Chris McAllister's DFV-engined Gulf Mirage. Later, still dripping sweat, Redman headed for the weekend prizegiving party. 'That was a proper race', he beamed, 'I really enjoyed that. . .' Ditto.

Terry Stinnett of Alamo, California, took his 1960 Lotus 18 Formula Junior to a resounding 23rd place from 23 starters in race 4 on Sunday.

Philip Walker and Richard Attwood, seen here at Spa, rounded off a fine Lister Jaguar winning streak at Snetterton

AUTUMN

By this time of year, the racing action around Europe
and America is starting to wind down towards winter,
but there are still plenty of events on the fringes of the
classic car world, and this year, one of the most famous of
all was celebrating its centenary

5-6 October

Snetterton took its turn in hosting a full card of classic rac-
ing. The Norfolk circuit was wet and windy so no surprises
there. It was the final round of the Groveair Challenge and
the three-hour race was won by the duo of Philip Walker and
Richard Attwood in the Lister Jaguar who finished a couple
of laps up on John Harper's Cooper Monaco, and a further
two laps ahead of the Mike Wilds Lotus Elan. That meant
the Lister had won all three Groveair rounds for 1996. In
other races Chris Fox's Lola T240 took the Historic
Formula Racing Championship race, Paul Stafford's 240Z
the 1970s Road Sports race, and Mike Wilds the Sport
Racing Championship round in a Chevron B36 while
another Chevron, the Michael Schryver/Simon Hadfield B6
took the HSCC One Hour enduro.

20 October

Lotus apparently gets an unexpected new owner as Romano

Artioli came to a quick agreement with Proton Chairman
Yahaya Almed. The Malaysian company is reported to have
taken an 80 per cent share in Group Lotus worth £51 million
leaving Romano Artioli with 20 per cent worth £13 million.

30 October

Craig Breedlove crashed at 675mph while attempting to
break Richard Noble and Thrust's World Land Speed
Record. Remarkably his car, which was blown over by a gust
of wind and slid for four miles, was only lightly damaged
and Breedlove himself was unhurt.

3 November

The annual London to Brighton run didn't enjoy the best
weather but that didn't stand in the way of the celebrations.
It was 100 years since the Emancipation Day Run that set
the motor car free of its shackles in the UK, and a little rain
was not going to spoil that.

Not quite frozen solid at the end of the centenary run, 1903 Renault, on right, has found a couple of cousins

Earlier in the day and, just, earlier in the century - 1902 Renault leaves London ahead of campatriot from Panhard et Levassor

A hundred years ago, almost to the day, as the Emancipation Day Run passed through Reigate and the town came out to watch

Beaulieu's November firework spectacular, left, follows September's autojumble, above

Beaulieu's Year

There's a lot more to Beaulieu than just the National Motor Museum. Events are held throughout the year, culminating in one of the world's largest and most popular autojumbles

Drive through the New Forest in the region of Lymington and Lyndhurst on a certain weekend in early September, and you are certain to see an unseasonably large number of foreign number plates attached to cars going in or around your direction. Most will be Dutch or German and their destination will be Beaulieu - or more precisely the National Motor Museum and the Beaulieu Autojumble and Automart, an event which is now famous the car world over.

But although the Autojumble's fame outranks any other single draw at the National Motor Museum, it is just one of a huge number of varied events there, and Beaulieu's year is a fascinating one. A lively one, too. The word museum too often evokes a yawning image of static exhibits doomed never to move from their final resting place, their day well and truly done. But if that cliche still applies in too many cases, the National Motor Museum certainly isn't one of them. Beaulieu's guardians have known for many years that its 'living' events and displays

are what draw people through the gates, and for them this year's busy programme started with the Victorian Motoring Extravaganza which was held in early May.

Why Victorian? Well, the British Motor Industry celebrated its centenary in 1996, and this was Beaulieu's way of marking the occasion. With joint organisers the Veteran Car Club, Beaulieu put a typical amount of effort and enthusiasm into attracting not just any old Victoriana but the correct, mobile Victoriana.

As a result, almost sixty authentic pre-1900 vehicles turned up on Spring Bank Holiday weekend, to follow a series of routes around local Forestry Commission roads. There were driving tests (won by Noel Holbrook's 1899 Peugeot from Stan Greenaway's 1899 Century Tandem), there was croquet on the Palace House Lawn, and a brass band. And if some of the oldest vehicles were actually replicas, few could really object to a chance to see the incredible Trevithick London Steam Carriage, or Robert Ames' faithful recreation of the pioneering Benz.

There was plenty at Beaulieu's next event, too, that

It looks as though it's the right one. . . A typical autojumble pause for thought, above. Mary Monatgu takes the tiller of the Benz replica trike, right

looked old enough to be Victorian but wasn't. The annual autumn autojumble is so popular that Beaulieu now holds another in early June, and inevitably the bargain hunting Dutch were at that one too. On the sidelines, you could watch action such as the TR Register's demonstration of TRs from 2 to 8, or you could simply shop. And if you couldn't easily find what you needed, you could publish your needs or offers on a card on Classic Car Weekly's ad-wall - a huge, free bulletin board which was a clever touch from the event's sponsors.

The National Motor Museum caters for two-wheelers too - perhaps not as many as it would like and slightly tucked away upstairs, but they're there. So for the past two years, Beaulieu has also hosted an event called Motorcycle World, and although this July lacked the perfect weather of 1995 the number of trade stalls had more than doubled and over 2000 people turned up to see the likes of Sammy Miller and Phil Read, some spectacular Triumph racing triples and Len Vale Onslow, billed as 'Britain's oldest motorcyclist and workman'. Beaulieu being Beaulieu there was naturally an extensive 'bikes and bits autojumble as well.

And still talking of autojumbles, next up was the big one. Over the weekend of 7 and 8 September, a truly staggering num-

Star of the May Victorian Extravaganza was without a doubt Tom Brogden's wonderful replica of the 1803 Trevithick Steam Carriage

You just have to know what you're looking for at the Autojumble. Is there any point buying the lamp with the broken glass? Perhaps a new glass is as hard to find as the lamp itself

ber of automotive pilgrims in search of mechanical salvation descended on Beaulieu's grounds. This year's was the thirtieth, and bigger than ever, but who on earth makes up this massive herd? There can hardly be this many people restoring cars in the whole of Britain, and even taking into account numbers swelled by the odd ferry-load of acquistive visiting continentals, drawn by a weak pound to pick over the old bones of our bygone motor industry, the attendance is remarkable.

It doesn't even seem to matter whether it's wet or dry. This year the sun broke through and thankfully there was no slithering around to be done, but even when it rains and the huge grass encampment turns to mud, people circulate determinedly.

Curiosity and a strange fascination with old, often broken mechanical bits brings in many who have no clear intention of buying anything. And even if they go away at the end of the day without a single purchase, they still feel an inexplicably vicarious satisfaction and the knowledge that if perhaps they did actually need something one year, they might well find it.

Part, perhaps nearly all, the fun is in looking. Organisers and stall holders alike know this too of course, so as in any decent treasure hunt, your quest is made more difficult. In the case of the Autojumble that purpose is served by the vast amount of - I'm afraid there's no gentle way of putting this - old junk that clutters the place. That serves two purposes, the fun of complicating your search as you try to look beyond it, and the way it puts anything serviceable that you do find into a far better light. All around you is stark evidence of how far metal and machinery can degenerate and your relief at finding someting relatively unscathed is, if not unbounded, at least enough to make you more likely to buy it.

It's just the fun of the fair. If there is a genuine complaint you can level at the Autojumble it's that it is becoming a victim of its own success. Prices on some stalls are high and you have to look far harder for the many real bargains than maybe you imagined. There's nothing Beaulieu can do about that; you can hardly introduce price fixing for 1920s Alvis speedos or TR2 trim, you must let supply and demand fight it out in the time honoured way.

What Beaulieu does offer is the very real opportunity of finding just what you need and the organisers do what they can to help. There's even a tent in which to leave your larger buys while hunting for smaller ones, and the always incongruous sight of a Bureau de Change set up in the middle of a field.

If you're after cars themselves, alongside the Autojumble, the Automart has grown year by year. It's your chance to cash in on the huge, circulating, captive audience who just might want to buy your car. It's a rather less structured operation than the Christie's auction which always features on Autojumble weekend, but like so many other Beaulieu events, it can be big fun.

Even with its busiest weekend of the year out of the way Beaulieu doesn't shut up shop and wait for next year, readying itself instead for the huge Firework Fair in November. And when the National Motor Museum is not organising its own events it is quite likely to be playing host to any number of others. April saw both the Alfa Romeo Rally and the Granada MkII Rally call in, followed in May by the Lotus 7 and Jaguar Drivers Clubs' events, with the RS Owners, Mini Cooper Register and Austin 750 Motor Club hot on their heels, and with MGs and BMWs to follow through the next couple of months.

The range is enormous and this year was the perfect example, with everything from those belching Victorian steam carriages to screaming 3.5cc two-strokes in the World Championships for one eighth scale off-road radio controlled cars. And with the 'Hearse of the Year' show in between, celebrating 100 years of British coachbuilt hearses, Beaulieu's year had barely a dull moment.

For the second Donington round, Mike Littlewood switched to the ex-Gilles Villeneuve Ferrari 312T5 - with great effect

DONINGTON FIA CUP 1 September

It was back to Donington for round five of the FIA Cup and this was where Bob Berridge's good run came to a painful and abrubt halt. He had been going brilliantly, fast enough to take pole position at over 110mph, in fact, but in the final qualifying session he tangled wheels with Ean Pugh's Brabham BT34, flew into the air and smacked into the pit wall. Berridge hadn't had time to remove his left hand from the steering wheel and his thumb and wrist were badly broken.

Berridge, naturally, was out of qualifying, out of the race and apparently out of the championship - but remarkably his wounds would mend in time for the trip to the Czech Republic. In his absence, his Empress Racing team-mate Steve Hitchins took the first place in the field of 26 cars on the grid, ahead of Geoff Farmer's Tyrrell. Mike Littlewood had won the first round of the series when the cars were last at Donington and he was in the frame again on the return to the circuit for this penultimate round in the championship. He was fourth on the grid, this time in the ex-Gilles Villeneuve Ferrari 312T5 rather than the proven race-winning Williams FW07.

It would have needed Villeneuve himself to keep ahead of Martin Stretton, though, who made the perfect start from the row behind Littlewood, his Tyrrell 005 rocketing ahead of the Ferrari into third. After seven laps the enormous pressure that Stretton exerted on Geoff Farmer paid off, helped by the fact that Stretton's older car actually seemed to be far better set up. When Farmer finally ran too wide on one corner Stretton was through but unfortunately for him Steve Hitchins was not in the mood to make any mistake whatever the pressure. That pressure did tell in the end though - with less than four laps left it was all too much for the Tyrrell's engine, and the expiring Cosworth prompted Stretton to spin off into the sand at Coppice.

That left Farmer in the Tyrrell to finish second, some seven seconds adrift but with Martin Schryver's Lotus 72 yet again winning his class (while also setting a lap record) he had the championship won even before the last round in the Czech Republic.

The grid for round five of the FIA Cup was 26 strong. There would have been even more but for Bob Berridge's crash. Martin Stretton gave Steve Hitchins, below, a tough time until his Tyrrell expired

It's not all 911s MGBs and Lotus Cortinas in the historic rallying ranks. Christian Bauer and Michaela Riedl add welcome variety with Steyr Puch version of Fiat 500

MANX HISTORIC RALLY 12-14 September

So September arrived and with it the annual trek to Ireland's annexe in the Irish Sea - the motor sport mad Isle of Man, where the Manx Historic was again a Demon Tweeks/Classic & Sportscar round as well as earning Tarmac Historic points, and the top crews were gunning for results.

Regular 911 men Keatley and Nutt were joined in the Porsche ranks this time out by local star Andy Kermode, the Manxman having forsaken his ultra-quick Mini for this home event in favour of some heavier Stuttgart metal.

Unfortunately, though, his 911 sustained a puncture early on and in turn broke a shock absorber, which left Kermode to drive two stages in this condition before it could be replaced. And this time it was Dessie Nutt's turn to play the Good Samaritan, lending the islander a replacement in spite of the fact that they were fighting each other for second place at the time.

The Cortina battle was this time being fought out between David McErlain and Neil Calvert, and it was the latter who handed the class win to the former when his Lotus snapped not one but both driveshafts - only for McErlain to waste the advantage by throwing his own car off the road a matter of only yards from his stricken rival. C'est la vie. . .

So with this his third win of the season, John Keatley clinched the 1996 Tarmac Historic Championship in style. And the cheery, fun loving champion was justifiably thrilled by the achievement, on the strength that he had driven impeccably all season in terms of both pace and consistency. His Manx win took him ahead of Jimmy McRae in the Demon Tweeks/Classic & Sportscar reckoning too - leaving him at this late stage of the season as favourite to score a fine winning double.

McErlain and Merifield almost had Cortina honours in the bag after Neil Calvert broke both driveshafts - but threw the class lead away, almost within sight of their stricken rival!

7-8 SEPTEMBER

Spa Six Hours

What's the recipe for a perfect historic race weekend? Well, some good cars for a start. No problem there; Europe is full of them. Good drivers? Ditto. Perfect weather? Well it helps of course. Then throw in one of the world's greatest racing circuits, and there's none better than Spa, in the midst of spectacular Ardennes scenery and just before summer turns to autumn - and the recipe is complete. Or is it?

There's one more magic ingredient. Spectators. It does help to have a crowd. Without one the party all goes just a little flat. Sad, then, that no one seemed to have told the Belgians that the Spa Six Hours was taking place this year - assuming the locals aren't so blasé they won't watch anything slower than F1 here.

In fact for Saturday practice there were no spectators at the circuit whatsoever. And clearly none had been expected; there wasn't even a printed programme. Commentary boomed from the PA and echoed endlessly through the hills and trees as it does at Spa, but today there was no-one to hear it in any of its three languages. Even the advertising hoardings had gone after the recent Grand Prix, leaving only the inevitable Stella Artois signs to contrast with the even more ubiquitous pines.

If Spa was a ghost track, it was a friendly one, and the Six Hours was as informal and low key an event as you're likely to find; but you don't go to race tracks to relax. You go for the adrenalin rush, the buzz and excitement and the signs were not good.

The final straw would have been empty grids, because Spa is so huge that it needs either F1 speeds to keep the cars coming round regularly enough, or else great numbers to fill the track. In the latter respect, at least, here the organisers had with, one or two exceptions, excelled themselves. For the main event there were 69 cars; but even that turnout was beaten by the Squadra Bianca/ Trofeo Alfa Romeo race - which boasted no less than 75 entries. That really was enough to make the place look busy.

With two absolutely packed grids good racing should have been guaranteed and the Alfas duly delivered. The dozen Brits (including Alfa Owners Club chairman Ed McDonough in a Minari) were out of it, as were most of the others as German driver Olivier Grossel and one of the 47 Dutchmen, Ron Simons, streaked away from the pack in their two Alfettas. Grossel's turbo and Simons' GTV6 swopped the lead for lap after lap. They were quick enough to be lapping other cars after just five laps, a remarkable achievement considering that it's more than four miles around 'this roller coaster circuit' as the commentator rather quaintly put it. Gallingly for the Dutchman, when the music stopped it was Grossel who found the chair.

Ed McDonough provided a perfect illustration of the low-key nature of the event. He only managed one practice lap before the drive disappeared on his Minari. And one lap is definitely not enough laps to qualify, here or anywhere. Arguments ensued but the officials were only going through the motions, in the end just letting him get on with it, after getting him to sign a note saying he could drive and that he knew his way around the circuit. . .

Not everyone likes to overload on Alfas though, and the Six Hours had the variety you'd expect from a field of 69. Thirteen 911s led the way. A reflection that Spa is just over the border from

At times there seemed to be more cars than spectators - Six Hours had 75 of them. Hadfield and Schryver's pole position B6 led them away but its radiator collected a stone

The Ward and Conoley TVR Griffith started from second on grid and scored excellent win from Belgian 911. It was the Griffith's second Six Hour win

Long-tailed Le Mans Alpine of Besson and Bianchi is well suited to the long sweeps and fast straights of Spa. Qualified only eleventh but chased leaders most of way

Not all the good battles were at the front. One-Hour Group 4 race made GTB pilot Dantinne work hard to take tenth from MG of David Brooker-Carey

Pretty little 'Bobtail' Cooper of Hoole and Laidlaw tails Pearson and Pennel's D-Type

Dennis Welch Healey ran out of brakes in a big way, dropping it from leading bunch to well down

Hoeperman's heavy metal Lola T70 has Haverland's March 74S breathing down its neck. March was quicker!

Germany perhaps? Well maybe, except that they all seemed to be run by either French or Belgian outfits; and they would be mixing it with seven big Healeys, a handful of Alfa Giulia Sprints and E-types, the inevitable MGBs, a couple of TVRs and a single Chevron B6 and Ginetta G4. Some intrepid Dutchmen even entered a Vauxhall VX4/90, presumably hoping to double this model's competition record at a stroke.

The Vauxhall clearly wasn't in with a shout in the overall scheme of things, but the Simon Hadfield/Martin Schryver Chevron certainly was. It had competed regularly at Spa in the late 1960s and early 1970s and in deference to its GT and saloon car opposition it was running here on treaded tyres.

Even so, it streaked away into what looked a commanding lead until it lost three laps. As the cars streamed through Eau Rouge some just clipped the kerbs, others took the rallycross route and inevitably stones were thrown on the track. One of them was big and sharp enough to hole the B6's combined radiator and oil cooler. But once that was replaced, Hadfield battled his way back through the pack from 19th to fifth and, with such a big field, as he explained, 'I had to start getting more aggressive to make up the time'. Sadly it was all for nothing in the end, as a lengthy pit stop - with much pushing and pulling at the rear suspension and the obligatory head scratching - ended with the diagnosis of a clutch about to break up.

The real delight in these wildly diverse fields is watching two cars which were never intended to race each other locked in combat. When an Austin Healey 3000 can hold off the determined efforts of a well-driven Lotus 23B for lap after lap, you wonder what's going on. Both had been in the leading group (and the Lotus would finish fifth) but this battle became academic towards the end of the six hours after the Healey made the day's most spectacular pit stop with its fraught driver shouting 'stop me, stop me!' to his bemused pit crew as the brakeless and smoking car sailed past them. Spa had taken its toll on the rear brakes. All that was left of one pad was a smoking plate with a hole through it. A puff from the fire extinguisher, some burnt fingers then furious pumping and brake bleeding all took time and 'Bulldog', the Dennis Welch racing Healey, was well down.

With the Chevron also out of the way it was Joe Ward and Chris Conoley's immaculately prepared and beautifully driven TVR Griffith which won, ahead of the Belgian trio of Pirenne/Parmentier/Menage in a 911. The Griffith clearly knows its way around Spa; it's the second time it's won this race.

The huge entry virtually guaranteed the Six Hours would be a success but some of the other races where the grids were smaller inevitably fell slightly flat. In theory the Group 4 One-Hour Endurance should have been worth travelling to see, for thundering Lola T70s mixing it with the nimble Chevrons. But despite a storming drive by Mike Wilds in his Chevron B31 - making up lost time, setting fastest lap and almost catching the winning Beurlys/Deuz Lola T286 - there just weren't enough cars to make it look totally convincing. And the incongruity of Jim Gathercole's standard looking black MG Midget amongst the monsters and being lapped six times, simply heightened the air of unreality. So did the efforts of Belgian Ferrari 308GTB driver Dantinne to hold off the other Midget, driven with the utmost determination by David Brooker-Carey.

So you leave the Six Hours with mixed feelings. It's great to be at Spa, and the drivers clearly love the experience; but it really does need more people and more atmosphere to make it work even better. If only the numbers and the enthusiasm of a Goodwood or Coys Festival crowd could be transplanted to Belgium for the weekend, then Spa would be really special. . .

Dutch pair Wellink and Bronsgeest were nothing if not optimistic with VX4/90; and it wasn't slowest in race - quite

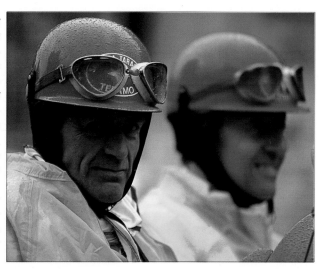

20-22 SEPTEMBER

Grand Prix Nuvolari

Find it impossible to get into the Mille Miglia? It's hardly surprising, but if that's the case you could try joining the Scuderia Tazio Nuvolari, and then you could enter the Gran Premio Nuvolari; it's not a bad substitute. This homage to the great driver has been taking place, appropriately enough around Mantua, since 1991. There was a Gran Premio Nuvolari well before that though; it was first held in 1954, just a few months after Nuvolari himself died; and then in the last four years of the real Mille Miglia, the GP Nuvolari prize went to the fastest driver between Cremona, Mantua and Brescia. It's a bit different now - as a celebratory rally open to pre 1973 cars.

The Scuderia itself was formed in 1993, in honour of the great man and it now has 35 members, most of them from Germany but with the likes of British Bentley driver John May making it a truly European club.

With the GP taking place in September, when conditions in the mountains are already getting tricky, normal people would take the simplest, quickest route south from Germany - especially if their car had been built 60 years ago. The Scuderia is not formed from normal people though, as president Peter Groh admits: 'Everyone could go on the highway, it's just too easy. We do it the hard way'. And the hard way means that they drive the likes of their Alfa Romeo P3, Aston Martin Mk II, Bentley 4.5-litre, Bugatti 37, Lagonda V12 and MG K3, to list but a few, over 600 kilometers, up through the mountains.

Drivers started out from Lake Bodensee on the German-Swiss border with the very first words in their road book making ominous reading: 'You have been warned. . .' Starting under a perfect blue sky, this may have sounded melodramatic but the crews regarded the warning in a different light as they tried to climb the 2578 metres of the Stelvio pass. By this time it was well into the night, the fog dropping visibility down to ten metres. 'This car was built for open roads and racing, not for a mountain trial', grumbled Magdalena Strecker as she tried to get her 1935 Aston Martin MkII around one of the Stelvio's 87 corners.

It's the middle of the night before Herbert Feierabend from Wurzburg arrives at the hotel at the top of the pass in his BMW 328. Why the delay? 'I wanted to do the GP in a Fiat Balilla but it broke down half way here so I had to go back and take the 328'. That didn't break down, but then Herbert is a BMW specialist.

The GP itself doesn't get underway until the evening in Mantua, and at 10.30 the Piazza Sordello is packed with spectators, just like the Mille Miglia, waiting to see the 160 cars start their first stage, three laps through the town and even in that an Italian team made the fatal mistake of following a lost Porsche until both had to turn around at the same place, each losing vital minutes. Most of the crews are from Italy and take the regularity trial far more seriously than the British and German drivers.

Day two is a different matter, as the cars are sent through small mountain roads through the mountains around Lake Garda, and now it's raining - not that the drivers care. The spectators seem to though, commiserating as they hand over coffee and cakes in the villages. The Italians are still serious, the rest just want to have fun. 'I don't have a speedo or a watch - I even lost my road book somewhere, so now I have to follow either the signs or the other cars', laughs Alfa P3 driver Robert Fink. 'The first fifty places usually go to the Italians but that's not important', declares Peter Groh who is driving the P3 that took Carlo Pintacuda to victory in the 1935 Mille Miglia. 'The important thing is the atmosphere. A race like this can only be held in Italy. In Germany or Switzerland they would kill you'.

The last day takes the cars to Castl d'Ario, the small village where Nuvolari was born in 1892 and in front of his house his cousin Milada inspects every team. Now 78 years old, she has the same message for each of them, 'I'm proud that you take part'. At the end of the day the Italian Franciosi duo and their tiny Giaur Taraschi 750 Sport are given the Gran Premio Nuvolari for 1996.

That's not the end for the Scuderia Tazio Nuvolari though, They pack themselves in their waxed cotton and head back through the rain to Lake Garda; and in Salo they have a party to celebrate Nuvolari which would have made even the Bentley Boys proud, before heading back over the mountains in the rain.

In spite of the cheery waves, the crew of this 1938 BMW 328, right, finished a long way out of contention. Best placed of this year's four 328s was Cane and Galliani in tenth place

Even with a blower, the mountain climbs can be hard going. This is Wendel's 1935 MG K3, breathing hard, left. Police in Italy don't care how fast old cars go, but do they know where the other cars went?

MG crew find local carabinieri friendly, and unconcerned about such mere trifles as a speed limit. Nuvolari epitaph reads 'You will travel faster still upon the highways of heaven'

You couldn't have a homage to Nuvolari without an Alfa Romeo. This was one of 14 on the rally, and as the oldest of them, one Nuvolari himself could have known

TARGA ESPANA *16-19 September*

The second Targa Espana repeated the success of the first, held in 1995, and once again, organiser Phillip Young had got it just right. The Targa is open to pre-1968 saloons and sports cars, with a special touring class for pre-1950 models, and this year more than sixty eligible cars were attracted.

There was the inevitable cluster of MGBs, of course, with the likes of Ron Gammons and Paul Easter among the nine entered, and familiar rally stalwarts like Porsche 356s and Jaguar XKs; but here they were joined by some more unusual machines.

Mauricio Selci and Andrea Campagnoli opted for a Citroen 2CV, while Nigel and Paul Broderick entered something with even less of a competition record, a Ford Anglia Estate. Other more imaginative mounts were the Bristol 400 of Alexa Scott-Plummer and Gillian Goldsmith, Tony Davies and Alan Smith's Gilbern 1800GT and the Austin A90 of Mike and Margaret Abram. At least that would have the abundant torque needed to climb the mountains that lay ahead.

The British contingent started with an easy leg, on the Pride of Bilbao taking them to Bilbao for the 16 September start. From there it would get considerably more difficult. The route had been planned by John Davenport, who as erstwhile Competition Manager for BMC must have seen hundreds of the very best and knew exactly how hard to make it for the right mixture of challenge and enjoyment, with difficult navigation and fast road sections as well as awkward regularity sections.

Day one took the crews from Bilbao west through the Cantabrian mountains and on to Oviedo, the ancient capital of Asturias for the first of the two night stops. The next day was packed with two large loops to be completed, west and south west of Oviedo and then followed a 12-hour drive at night across the Picos. The next morning they were heading off to Montes de Bidasoa near San Sebastian a few miles east from Bilbao.

The finish was at the tenth century castle at Fuenterrabia another few miles further east along the coast, by which time Spanish driver Ignacio Sunsundegui and his co driver Colin Francis had stamped their authority firmly on the event. Their Mini Cooper S had nearly two minutes of penalties in hand over the second place crew of John Buffum and Neil Wilson in their Porsche 356 with Ron Gammons and Paul Easter third. It was Sunsundegui's second Targa win on home ground and followed other excellent results this year which have also included second place in the Monte Carlo Challenge.

Porsche 911 or big Healey are obvious choices for classic rallying, so it's good to see a perfect Lincoln, left. Sadly, though, Don and Bonita Saunders' car retired. Just as unusual was Roland D'Ieteren's Siata 208S, right, which did finish - in 15th

Michael Cornwell and Willy Cave were 17th in their Porsche 356, above. They finished a good few places above the newer 912, left, of Andres Miro and Victoria Romagosa

Roy Hatfield's Austin Healey 100M, left, was one of only three big Healeys on this the second Targa Espana

4-6 OCTOBER
Eifel Klassik

At the Eifel-Klassik, classic cars have the unique opportunity to compete on the historic Nürburgring 'Nordschleife', a circuit still regarded by many as both the finest and the most difficult in the world. Mike Reidner watched this year's events and his thoughts turned back to when there was real racing at the Ring. 'Jackie Stewart won the German Grand Prix at the Nürburgring three times, including the epic race in fog and rain in 1968 when he brought his Matra-Ford to the chequered flag a full three minutes ahead of Graham Hill's Lotus. He had his own expression for the Nürburgring and his words are still quoted today. 'Green hell'.

Stewart's remarks say a lot about the circuit in its classic form. Opened in spring 1927, the original Nürburgring wound its way through the dark Eifel forests - a tortuous, 16-mile long circuit with more than 175 bends, uphill and downhill, and even including a short stretch of banking in the famous Karussell.

Stirling Moss won the Nürburgring 1000km race four times, including twice with a works Aston Martin. In 1961 he also won the German Grand Prix here in Colin Chapman's Lotus. 'It was one of my most satisfying wins', recalls Moss today. In 1996 he came back to the Nürburgring as a competitor, for the first time in 35 years, teamed up with Jochen Neerpasch, in a Cobra Daytona Coupé in the ten-lap race for historic GTs and touring cars at the ninth Eifel-Klassik.

After his first few laps of practice, Moss was smiling. 'You know why they let us drive both the Nordschleife and the new Grand Prix circuit?', he said. 'It's because that's the quickest way to find out how boring that new circuit is.'

Also racing a Cobra this year was David Piper, who last drove on the classic race track in 1969, in the tricky Porsche 917. 'Von Hanstein took us to the paddock at six o'clock in the morning, most probably because he wanted to avoid the German drivers having any chance to tell us how bad the 917 really was at this stage of its career. We made it into fifth place, and in the end von Hanstein was so satisfied that our wages were doubled. Those were the days'.

And today? 'Well, the track has changed a lot since then. There are places you remember much as they used to be, but others have changed a good deal. The whole track is much wider and smoother, and all the ditches alongside the track have disappeared. Back in our day a car could leave the track, go through the ditch and disappear completely. Some were missing for ages! Today, after such a long time, I would need about twenty laps to learn the circuit again in all its detail. It is just so long, and before you come to the same spot again, eleven minutes have gone'.

Another famous driver, twice World Rally Champion Walter Röhrl, drove his third Eifel-Klassik this year, behind the wheel of an Austin-Healey 3000 MkII, and he is another big fan. 'I simply love this track', he says. 'If all the race tracks in the world had been like this, I would never have gone rallying, I would have gone racing'.

At the Klassik, the old cars are reunited with, as near as is still possible, the same track where they used to race as many as seventy years ago. For the Eifel-Klassik, famous parts of the old Nürburgring come to life again. And so do famous motor racing names, from Alfa Romeo to Veritas. It is a real test. In the regularity trial, cars and their drivers tackle the 17-mile circuit combining the old Nordschleife and the new Grand Prix circuit for thirteen laps. And even after that, you might hear lots of ques-

The Ring is exhilarating enough for the drivers; the sensations that the co-drivers must experience can scarcely be imagined, left and right

Stirling Moss, driving the ATS Cobra Daytona replica, sharing with Jochen Neerpasch, was seventh in his race and put up the second fastest lap (in 11min 6sec) to prove that even at 66 years old most of the magic remains

Steinlet's Austin Healey 3000 gets a final windscreen clean and wheel check before starting the race

tions around the paddock from drivers who are still trying to work out the best racing line in that one special corner that goes, you know, uphill and fast right, say about three quarters of the way around the old track.

Some drivers of the past also took their time to learn this monster. Jacky Ickx, eventually a profound master of the Ring, came here for a complete week in 1965 to learn the track by heart. And it payed off: in Grand Prix and F2 racing as well as in the 1000km races in the early 1970s, the Belgian Le Mans record winner was the one to beat in the Eifel mountains.

Ickx had this way to look at his attempts, 'Even after a good lap you remember a liitle mistake, so you try again to get

that elusive perfect lap and that's why you always come back.'

So do the participants in the Eifel-Klassik. They all come back. And it is a little like coming home. Of the more than 200 cars competing in the regularity trial more than seventy date from before World War II. An armada of green and silver Bentleys comes to the event every year to meet the red Alfa Romeo Monzas or the huge white Mercedes-Benz Ss and SSKs. And that's not to forget the compact racing Bugattis or the sturdy Lagondas.

At the Eifel-Klassik, motor racing history comes alive and for three days in early October the Nürburgring changes into a rolling museum, whatever the odds against. Think, for instance, of the typical, sometimes atrocious weather conditions in this

Tony Dron was one of this year's Eifel stars, winning his race against the father and son pair of Welch Austin Healeys in rare Ferrari 330LMB, *left* and *below*

'Old Mother Gun' wasn't built with the Nurburgring in mind - but Michael Rudnik gave it his best shot, up against the Mercedes SSKs, 13 other Bentleys, an Alfa P3 and even a Ford Model T racer

part of Germany: it can be fantastic but it can also be cold, chilly, rainy and foggy, with the sharp wind blowing right through to your bones. But the drivers had to take it, then and now. Maybe the most boring Eifel-Klassik weekend would be one with sunshine from Friday to Sunday.

'On a dry track anybody can drive - it needs rain and a slippery road to find out the masters'. Those words, spoken by the exhausted owner of a Mercedes-Benz S in 1927, the opening year of the Nürburgring, encapsulate the enthusiasm that the unique combination of classic cars on this classic track provokes. Next year there will be two birthdays: the Nürburgring itself turns seventy and the Eifel-Klassik will be ten. So let's celebrate both.

FIA CUP BRNO 28-29 *September*

Against all the odds, Bob Berridge was back in business for the sixth and final round of the FIA Cup - at Brno in the Czech Republic. His hand and wrist were in plaster after his Donington smash but that didn't stop him putting his repaired RAM on pole position for the second Bohemo GP.

Berridge got away first too, before being passed by John Fenning's Williams FW07 on lap two. His race would not last very much longer; second and third gears broke after the RAM had spun having jumped out of gear.

At that stage Berridge was about to be passed by Simon Hadfield, who had stepped in for Ermanno Ronchi to drive the Bernie Ecclestone Brabham BT49. With Berridge out of the way Hadfield put the pressure on Fenning, having already regained a place lost to Steve Hitchins' Lotus 78. Neither Fenning's Williams nor Hadfield's Brabham appeared long on grip but eventually Hadfield managed to get past and pull away to win by over seven seconds. A spin put Steve Hitchins out of contention but after his Lotus 78 was pointed in the right direction he recovered to finish fifth ahead of the second Brabham BT49.

With the championship already decided the pressure was now off Michael Schryver, which was just as well as the old Lotus 72 was feeling the effects of the latter stages of a hard season. To preserve its transmission, Schryver used only fourth and fifth gears and as Michael Schumacher had demonstrated last season good drivers don't need a full gearbox. The two-speed Lotus still finished ahead of Andrew Wareing's Williams FW06 for another class win and an even more comprehensive championship victory.

Consistent results in one of the older cars in the series deservedly gave Michael Schryver, above, the 1996 FIA Championship. Joaquin Folch's Lotus, right, leads the pack through the first turn at Brno

CCT OF IRELAND RETRO 11-13 October

This event tries to recreate the 1950s and 1960s Circuit of Ireland with the emphasis firmly on enjoyment. As expected some of the early cars (and some came from the 1930s) had mechanical problems early on for such a long (three days and 900 miles) rally but the organisers made provisoion for those crews to effect repairs and rejoin the rally at a later stage.

This year's event attracted 120 crews and the route took them from Newcastle Co Down then through the border counties to the Friday night stop in the Athlone area via the midlands and Tipperary, Cork and the Ring of Kerry. Sunday's final stage would be over famous old stages such as Ballaghbeama to the Dingle peninsula. However, any crews hoping to enjoy some spectacular scenery over some of the most challenging routes this side of the Stelvio were disappointed by torrential rain throughout.

The road rally and auto test fraternity traditionally dominate the competitive aspect of the event and the Hill-Scott/Isacc Burley Midget opened up an early but slim lead from Eric Patterson and Derek Smyth while behind them problems mounted for Kenneth Gray and Peter Stevens as they suffered steering failure in the TR2 and Arthur Clark's Jaguar suffered total brake failure but luckily found a gravel trap before disaster struck.

Saturday brought yet more rain and monsoon conditions as other crews began to make their mark, such as Rob Woodside and Colin Francis in a VW Beetle, and Eamon Bryne and Paul Phelan in a Cooper S, as cars aquaplaned and their electrics died.

By Sunday though, the top six were all still in with a chance, particularly Hill-Scott, Eric Patterson and Robert Woodside. Eamon Bryne was an outsider - but what an outsider, as he set the pace on the autotest and co driver Phelan had a steady run on the regularity. As the other contenders suffered problems and dropped away so Bryne and Phelan took the silverware.

Kenneth Gray and Peter Stephen were briefly sidelined by a steering failure on their Triumph TR2, until a local garage got them back in the rally

Torrential rain did its best to wash out the Retrospective but everyone, including Michael and David Armstrong, in an MG TD, rose above it

Eamon Bryne and Paul Phelan at Caislean, on their way to a fine victory, ahead of Robert Woodside's VW Beetle

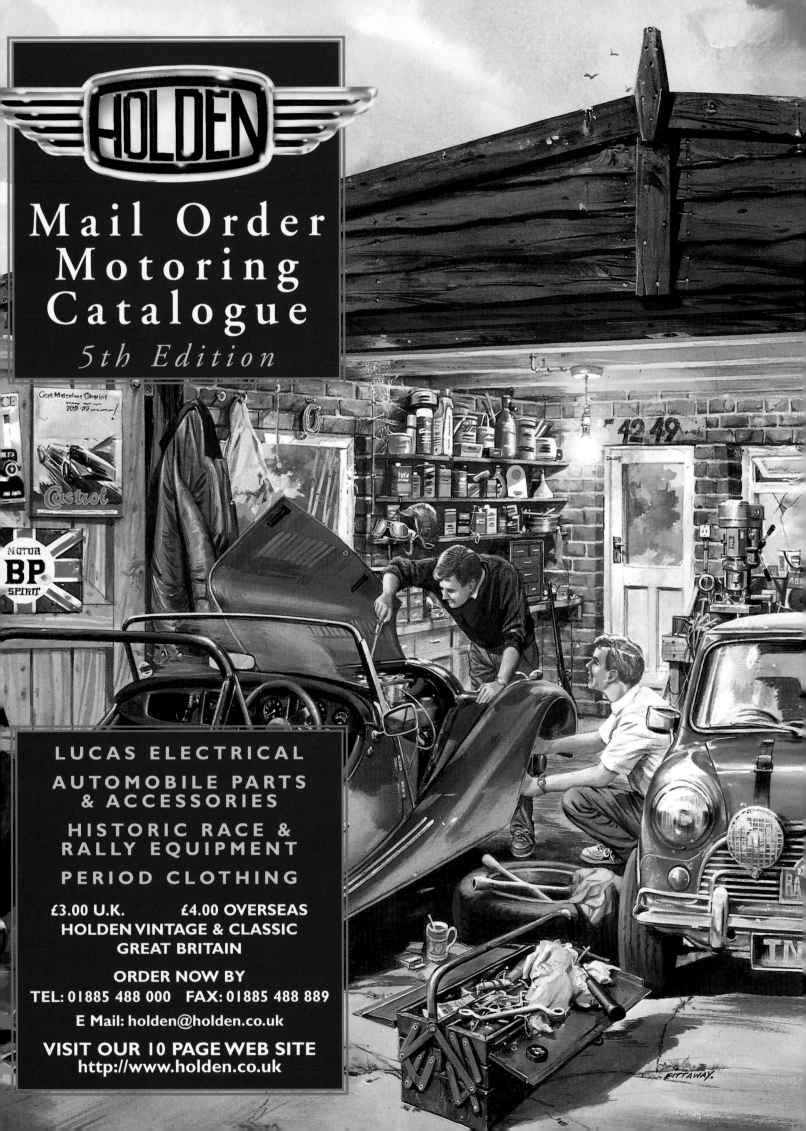

And finally...

*To all of you for whom this Casque cartoon hits too close to home
we hope repairs are successfully effected through the winter ready
for the next classic season, whether it be for the chill of the
Pomeroy Trophy or the glamour of the Tour de France Auto*

CREDITS

The Editor and the Publishers of International Classic Car Year 1996 gratefully acknowledge the assistance of the following individuals and companies who have contributed to the editorial and photographic contents of this book

EDITORIAL CONTRIBUTORS
Lord Montagu of Beaulieu, Kevin Brazendale, Peter Collins, Mark Gillies, Hans Jorg Gotzl, Brian Laban, Paul McIlroy, Richard Meaden, Mike Riedner, Peter Tomalin, Chris Willows

PHOTOGRAPHIC CONTRIBUTORS
Michael Bailie, Peter Barker, BMW (GB) Limited, Kevin Brazendale, Graeme Brown Photographic, Brent Bursan, Andy Christodolu, Clicksport/Mike Johnson, Peter Collins, John Colley Photography, Alan S D Cox, Ian Dawson, EMAP National Publications Limited, Foto Studio ZumBrunn, France Autodelta, Ford Motor Company, Wilfred Geerts, Haymarket Motoring Publications Limited, Historic Sports Car Club, Martin Holmes, Photo Jooss, Dave Kennard, Paul McIlroy/TPM Photosport, James Mann, Martin & Welsh Motor Racing Photographers, Bruno Muller, Reinhard Mutschler, National Motor Museum Beaulieu, John Overton, Marcus Pye, Eric Sawyer, Helmut Schnug, Colin Taylor Productions, Mick Walker, Chris Willows, Phillip Young